W0216203

ENGLISCH 1

blicken statt büffeln

Der Sprachkurs in spannenden Kurzgeschichten
für Anfänger mit Vorkenntnissen

bearbeitet von
Dorith Herfeld

PONS GmbH
Stuttgart

PONS

ENGLISCH 1
blicken statt büffeln

Der Sprachkurs in spannenden Kurzgeschichten
für Anfänger mit Vorkenntnissen

bearbeitet von
Dorith Herfeld

1. Auflage 2017

Autor der Geschichten 1-10: Dominic Butler
Autorin der Geschichte 11: Dorith Herfeld
Autorin der Übungen: Dorith Herfeld
Redaktion: Christina Cott
Logoentwurf: Erwin Poell, Heidelberg
Logoüberarbeitung: Sabine Redlin, Ludwigsburg
Einbandgestaltung: Ilham Widmann
Coverillustration und Büffel: Thomas Hartmann (Illustrathomas)
Cover Hintergrundillustration: Michael Luz, Stuttgart
Layout: PONS GmbH, Stuttgart
Satz: tebitron gmbh, Gerlingen
Druck und Bindung: Multiprint GmbH
ISBN: 978-3-12-562966-0

Welcome!

Sie haben schon Vorkenntnisse in Englisch und möchten Ihr Wissen unterhaltsam und entspannt aufpolieren? Sie wollen aber nicht wieder bei Null anfangen ... Dann starten Sie doch mit einer kurzen Geschichte! Lesen ist eine der effektivsten Methoden, um eine fremde Sprache zu erlernen. Wir haben für Sie hier elf kurze Geschichten ausgesucht, mit denen Sie Ihre Grammatik- und Wortschatzkenntnisse auffrischen und erweitern können. Ob Krimi, Liebesgeschichte oder Komisches: Mit unterhaltsamen Geschichten lernt es sich entspannter. Die Texte sind kurz und so lässt sich das Lernpensum gut an Ihre Bedürfnisse anpassen und Sie können auch unterwegs, im Zug oder im Urlaub, lernen.

Wie lernen Sie mit dem Sprachkurs?

Der Sprachkurs enthält 11 Lektionen. Auch wenn Sie schon Vorkenntnisse haben, empfehlen wir Ihnen, die Lektionen der Reihe nach zu bearbeiten, da die Themen, besonders die der Grammatik, im Laufe der Lektionen aufeinander aufbauen und sich im Schwierigkeitsgrad steigern.

Jede Lektion enthält eine abgeschlossene Geschichte und passende Übungen dazu. Je nach Geschichte haben wir diese in mehrere Abschnitte unterteilt.

Lesen Sie zuerst den ersten Abschnitt einer Geschichte. Die Erklärungen der schwierigsten Wörter am Seitenrand helfen Ihnen diese zu verstehen. Übungen zum Leseverstehen und zum Wortschatz unterstützen Sie dabei, die Geschichten weiter zu entschlüsseln. Die wichtigsten Grammatikthemen werden anhand von Beispielen aus den Geschichten aufgegriffen, erklärt und geübt.

So erschließen Sie sich nach und nach den Teil der Geschichte und können dann mit dem nächsten Abschnitt fortfahren - bis zum Ende der Geschichte. Nach und nach werden Sie so die Geschichte besser verstehen und haben so ganz ohne Büffelei Ihre Englisch-Kenntnisse wieder aufgefrischt und erweitert.

Am Ende des Buches können Sie die Lösungen zu den Übungen und schwierige Wörtern im alphabetischen Wortverzeichnis nachschlagen. Weitere Wörter können Sie auch unter www.pons.de kostenlos nachschlagen.

Viel Lese- und Lernvergnügen!

Ihre PONS-Redaktion

Im Kurs verwendete Abkürzungen:

Abkürzung	Bedeutung
so.	someone - jemanden
sb.	somebody - jemanden
sth.	something - etwas
AE	American English - amerikanisches Englisch
jmd.	jemandem
jdn.	jemanden
pl.	Plural - Mehrzahl

1. THE STRANGER

"Tickets?" says the **CONDUCTOR**.

I am alone in a small **COMPARTMENT** of an old **STEAM TRAIN**. It is midwinter and outside the evening sky is black. With a smile I take my ticket from the pocket of my coat and pass it to the conductor.

"**ALL THE WAY** to Whitby?" he asks. "Are you **STAYING** there for the night?"

"Yes," I reply. "A friend says they have the best fish and chips in England."

The conductor smiles. "It's true. And where are you from? That's not an English accent."

"Canada. I'm here on holiday **TO EXPERIENCE** some traditional English culture."

"In the middle of winter? Well, I **SUPPOSE** you Canadians like the cold. And where are you staying?"

"A small hotel near the **HARBOUR**."

"Ah, very good. You can see the **ABBEY** from the harbour. Well, enjoy the journey. This old steam train is not very fast, but it's certainly traditional."

The conductor closes the door to the compartment and I make myself **COMFORTABLE**. The compartment is not very warm, but I have a hot **FLASK** of tea in my bag. I take it out, pour a cup, then

conductor – *Schaffner*
compartment – *Abteil*
steam train – *Dampflok*

all the way – *den ganzen Weg*
to stay – *bleiben*

to experience – *hier: miterleben*

to suppose – *annehmen*

harbour – *Hafen*

abbey – *Abtei*

comfortable – *bequem*
flask – *Thermosflasche*

crossword - *Kreuzworträtsel*
to make s.o. feel tired - *jmd. müde werden lassen*

open my newspaper. The stories do not interest me, so I find the **CROSSWORD** and begin to complete it.

After some time, the slow rhythm of the old train begins to **MAKE ME FEEL TIRED**, so I close my eyes.

I sleep for no more than a few minutes, then a noise in the compartment wakes me and I scream in surprise.

to disturb - *stören*
tall - *groß*
pale - *blass*
curtain - *Vorhang*

"Excuse me," says the stranger. "I am sorry to **DISTURB** you."

He is a **TALL** elegant man with black hair, dark eyes and **PALE** skin. He is standing by the window of the compartment and I see that the **CURTAINS** are now closed.

"It's fine," I say, then I watch him sit down and look at me.

"You're from Canada," he says. "Ontario. Ottawa?"

suddenly - *plötzlich*
very awake - *hellwach*

"My God, yes, how do you know?" I ask, **SUDDENLY VERY AWAKE**.

He smiles and for a second I see his perfect white teeth. "I love to travel. Canada is one of my favourite countries, the people there are so … **WELCOMING**. They always invite me into their homes."

welcoming - *freundlich*
expression - *Ausdruck*

I think that I see a strange **EXPRESSION** on his face when he says this, but I do not understand why. "And you?" I ask. "Where are you from?"

1. A TRIP TO WHITBY

Haben Sie den Text aufmerksam gelesen? Beantworten Sie dann die folgenden Fragen. Mehrere Antworten können richtig sein.

1. Why does the narrator travel to Whitby?
- ❍ **A** To eat the best fish and chips in England.
- ❍ **B** To see the Abbey.
- ❍ **C** To experience English culture.

2. Who is the narrator?
- ❍ **A** An English tourist.
- ❍ **B** A Canadian tourist.
- ❍ **C** A Canadian businessperson.

3. The narrator feels ...
- ❍ **A** traditional.
- ❍ **B** comfortable.
- ❍ **C** tired.

4. The stranger has ...
- ❍ **A** black hair.
- ❍ **B** fair hair.
- ❍ **C** yellow teeth.

5. Why does the narrator scream?
- ❍ **A** He is threatened by the conductor.
- ❍ **B** He is woken up by a noise.
- ❍ **C** He is shocked by something he sees outside.

6. Where does the narrator stay?
- ❍ **A** In a bed & breakfast.
- ❍ **B** With friends.
- ❍ **C** In a small hotel.

Isst der Reisende wirklich Fisch und Kartoffelchips? Nein. Er isst Fisch mit Pommes Frites. Manchmal muss man aufpassen, ob man sich im UK oder den USA befindet, da es einen Unterschied zwischen American English und British English gibt. Manchmal sind es andere Wörter: So sagen die Briten **chips**, wenn sie von Pommes sprechen, die Amerikaner aber **French fries**. Manchmal ist auch die Schreibweise unterschiedlich: die Briten schreiben **favourite**, die Amerikaner **favorite**.

WITH A SMILE I TAKE MY TICKET FROM THE POCKET OF MY COAT AND PASS IT TO THE CONDUCTOR.

Lächelnd hole ich meine Fahrkarte aus meiner Jackentasche und gebe sie dem Schaffner.

2. TRAVELLING VOCABULARY

Unser Protagonist reist mit dem Zug. Finden Sie heraus, welchen Wörtern man bei einer Zugreise begegnen kann.
Ordnen Sie die Wörter den Bildern zu.

1

2

3
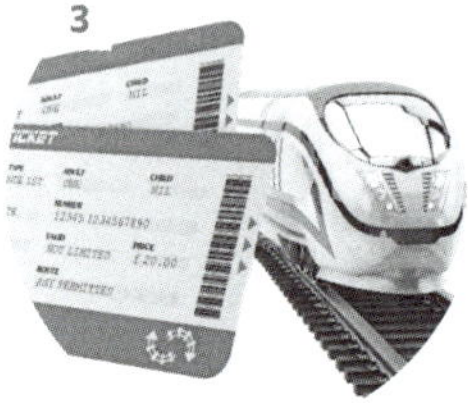

4

5
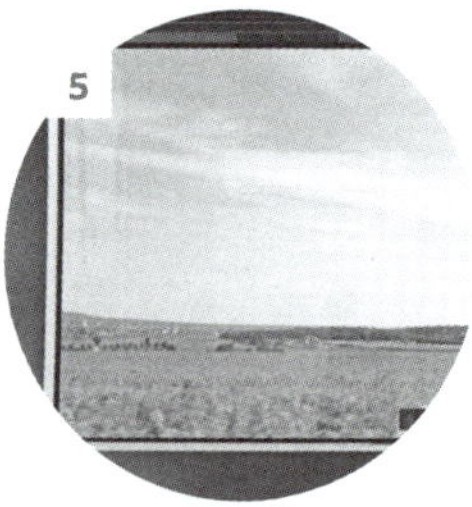

6

2 **A** conductor

3 **B** ticket

4 **C** old steam train

6 **D** curtain

1 **E** compartment

5 **F** window

3. WHERE ARE YOU FROM?

Kanada, was für ein schönes Land! Aber kennen Sie noch andere Länder? Tragen Sie die englischen Namen der Länder, die zu den entsprechenden Sehenswürdigkeiten gehören, ein.

1 Paris

2 Berlin

3 New York

4 [illegible]

5 China

6 London

Der Schaffner hat den Gast nach seiner Herkunft gefragt: **Where are you from?** Sie können auch so nach der Herkunft fragen: **Where do you come from?** oder **Where do you live?** – *Wo leben Sie?* Und so sagen Sie, woher Sie sind: **I am from Germany.** oder **I come from Germany.** ABER: **I live in Germany.** *Ich lebe in Deutschland.*

4. TO BE OR NOT TO BE

Wiederholen Sie eins der wichtigsten englischen Verben. Die Tabelle mit der Konjugation des Verbs *to be* ist unvollständig. Lesen Sie den Textabschnitt noch einmal. Suchen Sie die hier fehlenden Formen von *to be* und vervollständigen Sie die Tabelle.

to be

I am	we are
you are	you are
he / she / it is	they are

Füllen Sie jetzt den kleinen Text aus. Die Tabelle hilft Ihnen dabei:

The conductor asks, "Where **1.** are you from?"

The passenger **2.** I'm from Canada.

He **3.** is tired.

The stranger **4.** is sorry because he disturbed the passenger.

The passenger and the stranger **5.** are travelling to Whitby.

Neben diesen Langformen von **to be** kommen auch die folgenden Kurzformen in der Geschichte vor: **'m, 're, 's**. Diese werden oft in der gesprochenen Sprache und in informellen Schreiben wie E-Mails verwendet: **I am = I'm, you are = you're, he is = he's, we are = we're, they are = they're.**

Was hat es nun mit dem etwas rätselhaften Fahrgast auf sich? Woher weiß er, dass der Erzähler aus Kanada kommt?

"I'm from … Europe. Not England, but **I DO LOVE** this part of the world."

"Whitby?"

"Oh, yes. Whitby is very special to me. It is a place … very close to my **HEART**." And again I see that **STRANGE** expression and I want to ask him what is so funny, but I do not.

"So why do you like Whitby? Because of the fish and chips?"

And this time the stranger opens his mouth and laughs. "Oh no, my friend, I never eat … fish and chips."

Then for some time, the train moves across the cold English **COUNTRYSIDE** and we talk. He is a very **POLITE** and interesting man. He says that he speaks many languages and that he has houses in many parts of the world.

"And what is your **PROFESSION**?" I ask.

"I am a writer. A **GHOST** writer. I help other people write books."

"That's very interesting. Are the books famous?"

"Oh yes, one is very famous," he says with another smile. "Ah, do you feel that? The train is starting to slow. I think that we are near Whitby now. Tell me, my friend, would you like **TO JOIN** me for something to drink this evening? I am very **THIRSTY** after this long journey."

"Oh," I say. "Yes, why not?"

The stranger smiles at me. "Good, that's very good. But first you must see the Abbey."

"Oh yes," I say. "**MAYBE** we can see it from the train." And I move my hand to the curtain and open it.

I do love - *ich mag … sehr*
heart - *Herz*
strange - *seltsam*
countryside - *Landschaft*
polite - *höflich*
profession- *Beruf*
ghost - *Geist*
to join sb. - *jmd. Gesellschaft leisten*
thirsty - *durstig*
maybe - *vielleicht*

to shout
- *rufen*

"No!" he **SHOUTS**. "Close it! Close it now! We can see the Abbey later."

But I do not close the curtain, because I see something very strange. The small **SEASIDE TOWN** of Whitby is in the distance. Above it, on a small hill, is the famous Abbey.

seaside town - *Küstenstädtchen*

It is not this, **HOWEVER**, that is strange.

however
- *aber*

No, it is the reflection in the window that I do not like. For a moment I cannot understand what is wrong. I can see my own face in the glass. I can see the town and the Abbey.

But I cannot see ...

"Ah," the stranger says, but this time he does not smile. "Maybe **WE SHOULD** have that drink now."

we should
- *wir sollten*

And the lights in the small compartment go out.

5. THE END OF THE TRIP

Haben Sie den zweiten Teil der Geschichte verstanden? Kreuzen Sie an, ob folgende Aussagen richtig oder falsch sind.

		RIGHT	WRONG
1.	The stranger is not from Canada.	☒	○
2.	The stranger loves fish and chips.	○	☒
3.	The stranger helps other people write books.	☒	○
4.	The stranger wants to look at the Abbey.	○	☒
5.	The passenger can see the face of the stranger in the window.	☒	○

6. DINGE BESCHREIBEN

Was haben Sie über den Fremden erfahren? Suchen Sie die Adjektive im Text, die dabei helfen, ihn näher zu beschreiben.

1. p<u>olite</u> *(höflich)*

2. i<u>nteresting</u> *(interessant)*

3. t<u>hirsty</u> *(durstig)*

Allerdings ist der Erzähler beunruhigt über das Bild, das sich im Zugfenster spiegelt. Unterstreichen Sie die Adjektive:

... on a small hill, is the famous Abbey. It is not this, however, that is strange. No, it is the reflection in the window that I do not like. For a moment I cannot understand what is wrong.

7. SIMPLE PRESENT

Im folgenden Abschnitt kommt die Grundform des Präsens, das *simple present*, mehrfach vor. Was fällt Ihnen bei der 3. Person Singular auf? Vervollständigen Sie die Regel.

"OH YES, ONE IS VERY FAMOUS," HE SAYS WITH ANOTHER SMILE.

„Oh ja, eines ist sehr berühmt", sagt er mit einem weiteren Lächeln.

"OH," I SAY. "YES, WHY NOT?" THE STRANGER SMILES AT ME.

„Oh", sage ich, „Ja, warum nicht?" Der Fremde lächelt mich an.

In der 3. Person Singular bildet man im **simple present** die Endung bei Verben durch Anhängen von **1.** s.

Merken Sie sich diesen altbewährten Spruch, dann sind Sie auf der sicheren Seite: **He / she / it - das „s" muss mit!**

Einige Besonderheiten gibt es aber noch. Finden Sie in den Sätzen unten jeweils die Endung der Verben und vervollständigen Sie mit Hilfe dieser Beispiele die Regeln.

He goes home. She does her homework.

Bei Verben wie **to go** und **to do** wird **2.** es angehängt.

She kisses him. The dog watches them.

Bei Verben, die auf **-s** oder Zischlaut enden, wird **3.** es angehängt.

He tries to understand.

Bei Verben, die auf Konsonant +**-y** enden, wird **-y** durch **4.** ies ersetzt.

8. SIMPLE PRESENT

**Wie lautet die Geschichte aus der Sicht des Fremden?
Setzen Sie das Verb in Klammern in der richtigen Form ein.**

"Oh yes, one is very famous," I **1.** say *(say)* with another smile. "Do you feel that? (...). I think that we are near Whitby now. Tell me, my friend, would you like to join me for something to drink this evening? I am very thirsty after this long journey." "Oh," he **2.** says *(say)*. "Yes, why not?" I **3.** smile *(smile)* at him.

9. THERE, THEIR ODER THEY'RE?

Achtung! Diese drei Wörtchen werden alle gleich ausgesprochen, bedeuten aber grundverschiedene Dinge.

there *(dort)* **There are a castle and a wall on a hill.**
their *(ihr, Possessivbegleiter)* **Their owner is a very old, mysterious man.**
they're *(sie sind)* **They're very impressive.**

**Können Sie sie auseinanderhalten? Versuchen Sie es einmal.
Setzen Sie das richtige Wort ein.**

The stranger points at the train window. **1.** There, out in the darkness, I can see a castle.
"Look at the walls," I say to him, "**2.** They're beautiful! Tell me, you write ghost stories and have visited many people.
Have **3.** their stories inspired you? The castle certainly has."

10. VERNEINUNG IM SIMPLE PRESENT

Lesen Sie nochmals den letzten Teil der Geschichte und finden Sie die drei verneinten Formen im *simple present*.

1. I do not close ...

2. I do not like

3. He ______

Im **simple present** verneint man mit **don't** + Verb:

I don't know.

Bei der 3. Person Singular verneint man mit **doesn't** + Verb:

He / she / it doesn't know.

Don't steht für **do + not, doesn't** für **does not**. Das **-s** bei der 3. Person fällt bei der Verneinung weg:

He asks.

Aber: **He doesn't ask.**

Schreiben Sie die folgenden Sätze als verneinte Sätze.

4. I see that strange expression on his face.

I don't see that strange expression...

5. I want to ask him what is so funny.

I don't want to ask him ...

6. The stranger smiles.

The stranger doesn't smile.

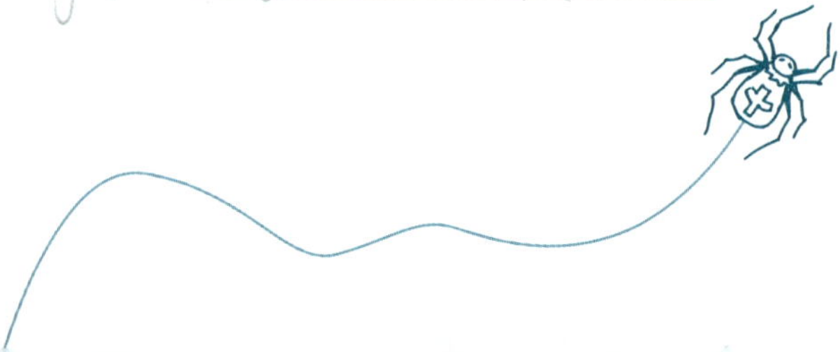

11. I CAN'T DO THAT

Jetzt sehen Sie sich noch an, wie man sagt, dass man etwas kann bzw. nicht kann. Suchen Sie hier ebenfalls die Beispiele in der Geschichte.

1. We can see the Abbey later

2. I do not close the curtain

Die verneinte Form heißt **cannot** oder **can't**. Achtung! Die 3. Person Singular wird ohne **-s** gebildet und heißt **he can** bzw. **he cannot**.

12. WHAT IS CORRECT?

Kreuzen Sie nun die Aussagen an, die mit der Geschichte übereinstimmen. Achten Sie dabei darauf, ob der Satz verneint ist oder nicht.

1. ○ A The stranger loves this part of the country.
⊗ B The stranger doesn't love this part of the country.

2. ○ A I open the curtain.
⊗ B I don't open the curtain.

3. ⊗ A The stranger speaks many languages.
○ B The stranger doesn't speak many languages.

4. ⊗ A I like the reflection in the window.
○ B I do not like the reflection in the window.

5. ⊗ A At the end of the story the stranger smiles.
○ B At the end of the story the stranger doesn't smile.

13. MY DEAR FRIEND. . .

"**My friend**" – *mein Freund* ... ob der Fremde wirklich eine Freundschaft zum Erzähler knüpfen wird? Sehen Sie sich die Possessivbegleiter an, d. h. die Wörter, die ausdrücken, wem etwas gehört. Sie stehen immer vor einem Substantiv, z. B. **my castle** – *mein Schloss*. Sehen Sie hier die Formen:

Possessivbegleiter

my	our
your	your
his / her / its	their

"IT IS A PLACE . . . VERY CLOSE TO MY HEART."

„Dieser Ort … liegt mir sehr am Herzen."

Setzen Sie nun im folgenden Text die richtigen Begleiter ein. Das Subjektpronomen in Klammern hilft Ihnen dabei.

The narrator thinks:

Oh, the stranger opens **1.** ___his___ *(he)* mouth and laughs at **2.** ___my___ *(I)* fish and chips. **3.** ___His___ *(he)* behaviour is very polite and **4.** ___his___ *(he)* houses are in many parts of the world. I wonder what **5.** ___our___ *(we)* conductor thinks about this man.

He asked me, "can I see **6.** ___your___ *(you)* ticket, please," but he didn't ask the stranger about **7.** ___his___ *(he)* ticket.

14. THE STRANGER

Haben Sie erkannt, wer der geheimnisvolle Fremde in der Geschichte war? Hier noch eine kleine Übung, die Ihnen dabei hilft, mit ein bisschen Smalltalk hinter sein Geheimnis zu kommen. Verbinden Sie die Fragen mit den richtigen Antworten:

1.	Why do you close the curtains?	**A**	I live in a castle.
2.	Where are you from?	**B**	I don't like sunlight.
3.	Where do you live?	**C**	I'm from Transylvania.
4.	How old are you?	**D**	My name is Count Dracula.
5.	What do you like to drink?	**E**	I'm hundreds of years old.
6.	What's your name?	**F**	My favourite drink is blood ...

Bram Stoker, der Autor des 1897 erschienenen Romans **Dracula**, erhielt seine Inspiration zur Person des Grafen während eines Aufenthalts in **Whitby**. Der Ort taucht auch im Roman selbst auf, denn eine der Heldinnen schreibt über die gigantische und gleichzeitig romantische und wunderschöne Ruine.

2. Always be Prepared

"So, Laura, what do you think?" Sam says as he stops the coach in the small seaside town of Marazion.

coach
– *Reisebus*

"Oh, Sam, it's wonderful!" says Laura. "What's it called?"

In front of them, a little distance into the calm blue sea, is a small green island with an old grey castle on top of it.

"St. Michael's Mount. Yes, it is quite impressive. I think the kids are going to like it."

quite impressive
– *ziemlich beeindruckend*

Behind them, six young scouts and six young girl scouts, all wearing brown scout uniforms and yellow neckerchiefs, are looking out of the window with big smiles on their faces.

neckerchief
– *Halstuch*

"Oh yes, what a fantastic idea. Do you know a lot about it?"

"No, but the guidebook says that there's a beautiful church next to the castle."

guidebook
– *Reiseführer*

"Oh Sam, you are clever," says Laura.

Sam, who is a very ordinary man with brown hair, looks at Laura, who is a beautiful young woman with blonde hair and blue eyes; and he blushes. "Oh, thank you, Laura."

to blush
– *erröten*

"And how do we get to it? Remember, we have to be back in Plymouth by seven o'clock, or there will be some very angry parents."

to get to sth.
– *etw. erreichen*

"There's a little causeway," says Sam, who points to a stone path that leads to the island. "It's only three o'clock now, we can walk across and have a look at the church and be back on the coach by half past four."

"Great! Come on kids, let's go and look at St. Michael's Mount!" says Laura, and she begins to lead the kids from the coach.

"Sam?" says little Harry, one of the young scouts. "Can I take the guidebook?"

"Oh, I don't think we need it, Harry."

"But the scout motto says 'always be prepared'," Harry replies.

"Oh no, we really don't need it," says Sam.

Then he and Harry follow the others to the causeway and carefully walk across the stone path, the cold blue sea on either side of them.

"Oh, it's fantastic. Shall we walk up to the church?" asks Laura when they reach the island.

"Yes, come on kids. Follow us!"

"Sam," little Harry says again. "There's a sign here. Do you think we should read it?"

Sam shakes his head. "No, I'm sure it's not important." ▶▷▶

causeway - *Damm*

motto - *Leitspruch*

prepared - *vorbereitet*

to carefully walk across sth. - *vorsichtig über etw. laufen*

shall we - *sollen wir*

sign - *Schild*

to shake one's head - *den Kopf schütteln*

1. Ein Pfadfinderausflug

Haben Sie den Text aufmerksam gelesen? Beantworten Sie dann die folgenden Fragen. Mehrere Antworten können richtig sein.

1. What is the castle called?

- **A** Marazion.
- **B** Mont-Saint-Michel.
- **C** St. Michael's Mount.

2. What does the castle look like?

- **A** It's a ruin.
- **B** Impressive.
- **C** The kids cannot see it. It's too foggy.

3. Why is Sam clever?

- **A** He knows everything about the castle.
- **B** He has a guidebook.
- **C** He has been there before.

4. How do the kids get to the castle?

- **A** They have to climb a mountain.
- **B** They have to follow a stone path.
- **C** It's right at the shore.

5. What is the scouts' motto?

- **A** Always help people.
- **B** Always come back.
- **C** Always be prepared.

6. Why doesn't Sam read the sign?

- **A** He thinks it's not important.
- **B** He doesn't see it.
- **C** He cannot read.

Scouts sind Jungen oder Mädchen zwischen 10 und 18 Jahren, die sich gerne in der Natur aufhalten, dort wandern, campen, Rucksacktouren machen und so weiter. Sie organisieren sich in **troops** und haben einen oder mehrere **troop leaders**. Sie sind damit die Entsprechung zu den Pfadfindern in Deutschland.

2. Farben

Die Welt ist bunt. Ordnen Sie die Farben den Sätzen zu.

green • brown • yellow • grey • blue • red

1. The grass is green.
2. The sky is blue.
3. A banana is yellow.
4. Sand is brown.
5. An alarm button is read.
6. A mouse is grey.

Welche anderen Farben fallen Ihnen sonst noch ein?

7. weiß – w______
8. schwarz – black
9. orange – orange
10. rosa – purbel

3. Eine Landschaft beschreiben

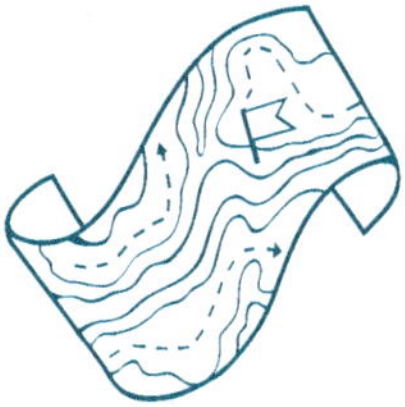

St. Michael's Mount ist wirklich beeindruckend. Finden Sie in der Geschichte die vier Begriffe, die die Kinder dafür verwenden?

1. wonderful *(wunderbar)*
2. impressed *(beeindruckend)*
3. beautyful *(wunderschön)*
4. fantastic *(fantastisch)*

4. To be a scout

Was braucht ein guter Scout alles? Ordnen Sie die Beschreibungen den Bildern zu.

1

2

3

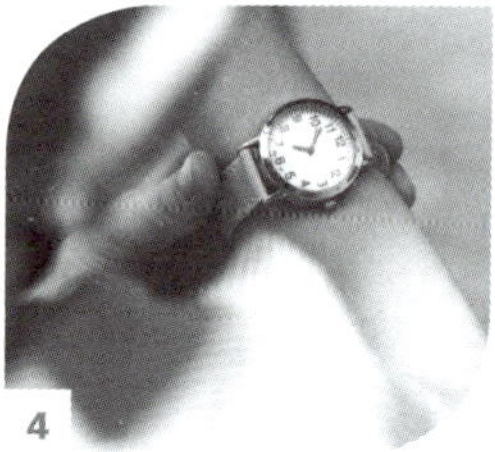
4

5

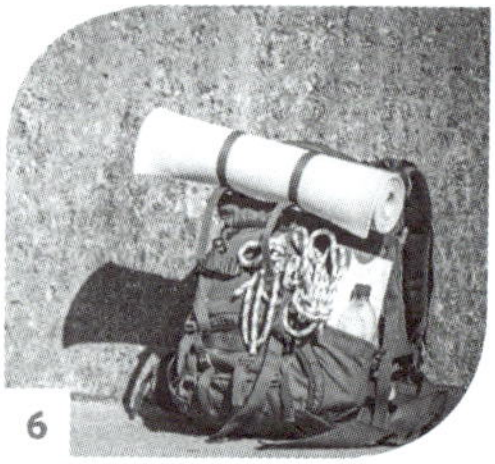
6

2 **A** neckerchief

6 **B** backpack

4 **C** watch

3 **D** map and compass

5 **E** hiking boots

1 **F** uniform

Achten Sie auf die zwei verschiedenen Worte im Englischen für Uhr: **watch** *(Armbanduhr)* und **clock** *(große Uhr)*, z. B. Wanduhr oder Kirchturmuhr.

5. Objektpronomen

Sehen Sie sich das Zitat an.
Us ist ein Objektpronomen, das auf die Frage *wem*? oder *wen*? antwortet. Sehen Sie sich alle Objektpronomen an.

"Yes, come on kids. Follow us!"

„Ja, kommt schon Kinder. Folgt uns!"

Objektpronomen

me	us
you	you
him / her / it	them

Auf dem Weg hat Laura ein wenig Zeit zum Nachdenken. Was denkt Sie? Vervollständigen Sie den folgenden Text mit den passenden Objektpronomen. Die Subjektpronomen in Klammern helfen Ihnen dabei, das passende Pronomen zu finden.

I am really happy Sam is here with **1.** us (*we*). I like **2.** him (*he*) very much. He always makes **3.** me (*I*) laugh. And he has great ideas. I also like little Harry. Actually, I like **4.** you (*they*) both, Sam and little Harry. They are very good friends.

6. Vorschläge machen

Lesen Sie im Text nach, was genau Laura vorschlägt, als sie auf der Insel ankommen, und vervollständigen Sie die Sätze.

Sie sagt: "**1.** Shall we walk up to the church?" Dann wird Sam von Harry gefragt: "Do you think we **2.** should read it?"

Beide Male handelt es sich um einen Vorschlag. Aber einer ist dringlicher. Entscheiden Sie im folgenden Beispiel, welche Anweisung die passende ist:

- [x] **A** You shall read signs when you are hiking.
- [ ] **B** You should read signs when you are hiking.

Shall und **should** bedeuten beide *sollen*, sind aber nicht austauschbar.

- Mit **shall** macht man einen Vorschlag oder verweist auf die Zukunft:
  Shall we go now?
  Sollen wir jetzt gehen?
  Shall hat aber auch Befehlscharakter und bedeutet dann *müssen*.

- **Should** ist höflicher und kommt einer freundlichen Aufforderung gleich:
  We should leave at five, so we don't have to hurry.
  Wir sollten um fünf losfahren, so dass wir uns nicht beeilen müssen.

7. Die Insel erkunden

Die Landschaft ist wirklich wunderschön. Lesen Sie sich die Beschreibungen durch und ordnen Sie sie dem passenden Wort zu.

In front of them, a little distance into the calm blue sea, is a small green island with an old grey castle on top of it.

Vor ihnen liegt, ganz nahe am ruhigen blauen Meer, eine kleine grüne Insel, an deren höchstem Punkt ein altes graues Schloss steht.

1. A place where you can talk to God.
2. A small mountain.
3. A large body of salt water.
4. A way made of stones.
5. Land surrounded by water.
6. A raised road or path that crosses open water or a wet area.

- **A** hill
- **B** stone path
- **C** causeway
- **D** sea
- **E** church
- **F** island

Im Text der Geschichte ist von **the English sea** die Rede. Gemeint ist damit das Meer vor England. Aufgepasst, das ist ein falscher Freund: **sea** *(Meer)* aber **lake** *(See)*.

Ob es weise war, das Schild nicht zu lesen? Vielleicht hätte Sam doch auf Klein-Harry hören sollen...

"But Sam, the scout motto...always be prepared," little Harry says, but Sam and Laura are already walking up the hill to the church.

"Hurry up, Harry!" Sam shouts when he sees the young scout reading the sign.

"Oh, it's very beautiful here," says Laura, looking at the blue sea.

to forget
- vergessen

"Yes, very," says Sam, who looks at Laura and forgets all about Harry.

to explore
- erkunden

Then, for the next hour, Sam, Laura and the scouts explore the small island, the church and the old grey castle.

lovely
- hübsch

"Well, this is lovely, but I think we have to go back to the coach now," Laura says.

Sam looks at his watch. "Yes, you're right. Come on kids, back to the coach," he says, and starts to lead the kids down the hill.

"How?" asks little Harry as they walk.

to mean
- meinen

Sam smiles. "What do you mean, Harry? We're going to walk across the causeway like we..."

terrible
- schrecklich

But then he stops, because in front of him he sees something terrible.

"What?" he shouts. "The causeway! Where is it?"

Because the little stone path is now completely underwater, and there is no way for them to cross the cold English sea.

"It's not here!" he shouts, then runs down to the sea and looks into the water.

"Oh Sam, what are we going to do?" Laura shouts.

"I...I...I don't know!" Sam says.

"But the kids, we need to get them back to Plymouth. The parents are going to be furious!"

It is then, however, that a small white boat sails up to where Sam is standing.

"Here you are, sir," the captain of the boat says. "Ready when you are."

"A boat? Oh Sam, you were joking! You are funny. How clever of you to organise a boat for us. Come on kids!" says Laura, and the scouts follow her onto the small boat.

"A…a boat?" Sam says.

"Yes," a voice behind him replies. "I spoke to the captain after I read the sign. You know, like the scout motto says…always be prepared."

And little Harry follows the other scouts onto the boat. ■

furious – *wütend*

however – *jedoch*

to sail up – *entgegensegeln*

to be joking – *Witze machen*

to reply – *antworten*

8. The end of the trip

Haben Sie verstanden, wie der Ausflug ausgeht? Kreuzen Sie an, ob folgende Aussagen richtig oder falsch sind.

	RIGHT	WRONG
1. Laura does not like the blue sea.	○	⊗
2. It's late, so they have to return to the coach.	⊗	○
3. The kids don't know the way back.	⊗	○
4. Laura believes that Sam organized a boat for them to take them back.	⊗	○

9. Das Present Progressive

In der Gegenwart verwendet man bei gewohnheitsmäßigen oder aufeinanderfolgenden Handlungen im Englischen das **simple present:**

... he shouts, then runs down to the sea and looks into the water.

...ruft er, dann rennt er hinunter zum Meer und schaut ins Wasser.

Bei Handlungen, die sich gerade ereignen, verwendet man das **present progressive**. Signalwörter dafür sind z. B. **while** *(während)*, **at the moment** *(in diesem Moment)*, **now** *(jetzt)*, **Look**, ...! *(sieh mal)*.

Können Sie anhand des Zitats die Regel für die Bildung dieser Zeitform vervollständigen?

Sam and Laura are ... walking up the hill to the church.

Sam und Laura laufen gerade ... den Weg zur Kirche hinauf.

1. Das **present progressive** bildet man mit:

einer konjugierten Form von to be +

Verb + ing.

Endet die Grundform auf **-e**, so entfällt es:

to come – I'm coming.

Was tun diese Personen gerade? Setzen Sie das *present progressive* der in Klammern angegebenen Verben ein.

2. Sam is shouting *(shout)*.

3. Laura and Sam are exploring *(explore)* the island.

4. I am speaking *(speak)* to the captain.

5. We are walking *(walk)* across the causeway.

10. Simple Present oder Present Progressive?

Versuchen Sie jetzt zu entscheiden, welche Verbform hier benötigt wird: *simple present* oder *present progressive*. Schreiben Sie die richtige Form des jeweils in Klammern angegebenen Verbs in die Lücke.

The kids **1.** walk *(walk)* up the hill and then

2. explore *(explore)* the small island.

Sam **3.** is looking *(look)* at his watch.

While he **4.** is checking *(check)* the time, the others

5. are seeing *(see)* something terrible.

The stone path **6.** is being *(be)* under water.

The kids **7.** are running *(run)* down to the path and

8. are looking *(look)* into the water.

Suddenly, Sam **9.** is seeing *(see)* a white boat.

He **10.** is saying *(say)*: Look, a man

11. is waving *(wave – winken)* at us – now we

12. are being *(be)* safe."

11. Nationalitäten

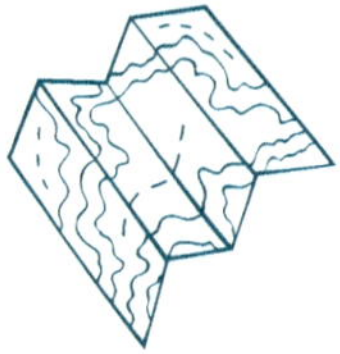

Wie heißen denn die Nationalitäten, die zu den Ländern passen? Ordnen Sie die Nationalitäten den Herkunftsländern zu:

Maltese • American • Czech • English • Dutch • French • Swiss • German • Italian • Scottish • Irish • Canadian • Polish • Russian

1. A person from England is... English

2. A person from the Netherlands is... Dutch

3. A person from Switzerland is... Swiss

4. A person from France is... French

5. A person from Italy is... Italian

6. A person from the US is... American

7. A person from Ireland is... Irish

8. A person from Scotland is... Scottish

9. A person from Malta is... Maltese

10. A person from Canada is... Canadian

11. A person from the Czech Republic is... Czech

12. A person from Russia is... Russian

13. A person from Poland is... Polish

And where do you come from?

14. I come from Germany, so I am German.

12. Aufforderungen

Suchen Sie die folgenden Aufforderungen im Text. (Tipp: für die 3. Aufforderung müssen Sie in den ersten Teil der Geschichte zurückblättern!)

1. H urry up! *(Beeil dich!)*

2. C ome on! *(Komm schon!)*

3. F ollow us! *(Folgt uns!)*

Was fällt Ihnen an der Befehlsform auf? Ergänzen Sie die Regel.

4. Das Verb steht immer in der Grundform,
das bedeutet, man braucht keine Endungen.

Welche Ratschläge kann man den *Scouts* erteilen?

5. Seid vorsichtig! — **A** Be careful!

6. Lest das Schild! — **B** Read the sign!

7. Schaut auf die Uhr! — **C** Look at the watch!

8. Keine Panik! — **D** No panic!

9. Seid allzeit bereit! — **E** Always be prepared!

Marazion ist eine wunderschöne Gegend in Cornwall. St. Michael's Mount ist quasi der kleine Bruder des französischen Mont Saint-Michel und war früher einmal eine Pilgerstätte. Wenn Sie einmal dorthin fahren, wissen Sie, wie wichtig es ist, die Schilder zu lesen bzw. an die Gezeiten zu denken!

3. The White Lady of Castell Coch

ghost - *Geist*
brave - *tapfer*
to dare - *sich trauen*
brace - *Zahnspange*
freckles - *Sommersprossen*
afraid - *verängstigt*
to lead to - *hinführen*
to whisper - *flüstern*
spooky - *gruselig*
to join the gang - *sich der Gang anschließen*

There was a **ghost** at Castell Coch; everybody knew that. Everybody also knew that only the **bravest** local teenagers from the town of Taff's Well **dared** to go there.

"I think we should go back home," Gwen said. She was a young girl of about thirteen, with light blonde hair, blue eyes and a **brace** on her teeth.

"We can't! You know we can't," said Mel, a taller girl with brown hair, **freckles** and a pair of red glasses. "Do you want the other girls to think we're too **afraid**?"

"But they won't know. We can tell them that we went to the castle. We can tell them we stayed there for a bit, that we saw nothing, then went home."

They were standing at the edge of a dark forest, their bicycles behind them on the quiet path that **led to** the town.

"But the other girls might be watching us, Gwen," Mel **whispered**. "You know, to see if we really go."

The two girls looked around, but saw nothing apart from the **spooky** trees and the pale moon in the dark night sky.

"Okay," said Gwen, "but just for a few minutes."

"No, you know the rules. If we want **to join the gang** we have to go all the way through the forest and touch the castle walls," Mel replied. "Come on, we'll be okay."

Slowly, they began to walk along a thin **trail** through the trees. The night was dark, but both girls were carrying small **torches** which they used to light the way.

"Mel, what does the ghost **look like**?" asked Gwen.

"Well, my brother Bryn says it's a lady. She's tall and thin and she always wears a long white dress. He said she lived in the castle, but one night her son walked into the woods and fell into a big hole and died. The lady was so sad that she died too, and now her ghost walks around the forest, crying and **moaning**, and looking for the boy."

Gwen **shivered**. "I think we should go back. I don't like this."

trail - *Pfad*

torch - *Taschenlampe*

to look like - *aussehen*

to moan - *stöhnen*

to shiver - *schaudern*

1. The ghost of Castell Coch...

Haben Sie den ersten Teil grob verstanden? Dann testen Sie es mal. Kreuzen Sie an, ob folgende Aussagen richtig oder falsch sind.

		RIGHT	WRONG
1.	A monster lives in Castell Coch.	○	○
2.	No one dares to go to Castell Coch.	○	○
3.	Mel has freckles and wears glasses.	○	○
4.	The girls drove to Castell Coch in a car.	○	○
5.	They went to Castell Coch during the day.	○	○
6.	They walked along a thin trail through trees.	○	○
7.	Mel's brother had told them about a white lady.	○	○
8.	The white lady killed her daughter.	○	○

2. False friends – falsche Freunde

Im folgenden Text fehlen einige englische Wörter, deren deutsche Übersetzung Sie vielleicht aufs Glatteis führt. Es handelt sich um sogenannte falsche Freunde. Das sind Wörter, zu denen es im Englischen ähnlich klingende Wörter gibt, die aber eine andere Bedeutung haben, z. B. a brave girl ist *ein mutiges Mädchen* (nicht ein braves!). Sehen Sie sich die Tabelle an und ergänzen Sie dann den folgenden Text.

Deutsch ▶	**Englisch**	**Englisch ▶**	**Deutsch**
Dessert	dessert	desert	*Wüste*
dezent	discreet	decent	*anständig*
Chef	boss	chef	*Chefkoch*
bekommen	to get	to become	*werden*
Gift	poison	gift	*Geschenk*
Prospekt	brochure	prospect	*Aussicht, Chance*
wandern	to hike	to wander	*ziellos umherstreifen*

Gwen and Mel **1.** ___hiked___ *(wanderten)* to Castell Coch.

They didn't **2.** ___wander___ *(umherstreifen)*, but followed the path.

They found a **3.** ___brochure___ *(Prospekt)* in the tourist information.

Later, they went to the local restaurant for a **4.** ___decent___ *(anständig)*

5. ___desert___ *(Dessert)*. Both liked the **6.** ___prospect___ *(Aussicht)* of good food before an adventure. Gwen's father was

7. ___chef___ *(Chefkoch)* there. She wanted to invite Mel as a

8. ___gift___ *(Geschenk)* for her birthday.

3. Ein Blick in den Spiegel

Die Teenager werfen einen Blick in den Spiegel. Was können Sie darin erkennen? Ordnen Sie die Wörter den Bildern zu:

1

2

3

4

5

4 **B** glasses

2 **A** freckles

3 **E** big blue eyes

5 **C** braces

1 **D** blonde hair

Wie sehen Sie aus? Füllen Sie die Kurzbeschreibung aus oder kreisen Sie die passende Antwort ein.

I am tall / small.

I wear / don't wear braces *(Zahnspange)*.

I wear / don't wear glasses *(Brille)*.

4. Allein im Wald ...

Zu gerne würde Mel ihrem Freund schreiben, wie mulmig ihr zumute ist. Leider ist sie so nervös, dass sie sich ständig vertippt. Was schreibt Mel da? Die Bilder helfen Ihnen dabei, den Wortsalat zu entwirren.

Gwen shivered. "I think we should go back. I don't like this."

Gwen zitterte. „Ich finde, wir sollten umkehren. Mir gefällt das nicht."

1

2

3

4

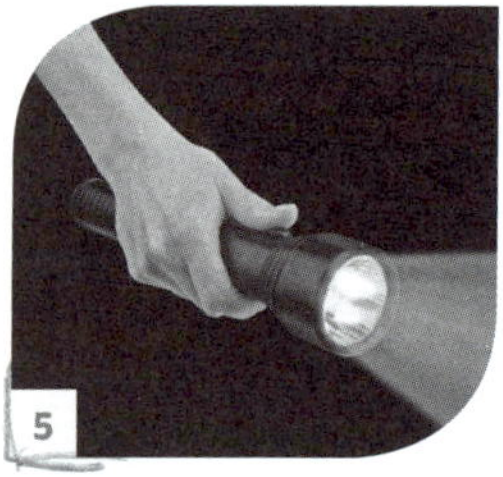
5

Hi Kevin,
Gwen and I are in a *rkad sterof* **1.** ____________________. All around us are *kospoy seetr* **2.** ____________________.
If you could just see the *lape nmoo* **3.** ____________________! We are walking under a *adkr ghtni yks* **4.** ____________________.
Thank God, I carry a *llams chrot* **5.** ____________________ with me.
I just hope I will see you again,
XXX Mel

5. Das Simple Past

Im **simple past** spricht man über Handlungen, die in der Vergangenheit abgeschlossen wurden. Es gibt im **simple past** regelmäßige und unregelmäßige Verbformen.

Können Sie bestimmen, welche der Verbformen in den Beispielen unten regelmäßig, welche unregelmäßig sind?

I walked home. **She walked fast.** **1.** regelmäßig

I went by bike. **They went to a club.** **2.** unregelmäßig.

Können Sie auch die Regel für die Bildung der regelmäßigen *simple past*-Form ergänzen?

Die **simple past**-Form von regelmäßigen Verben wird gebildet aus

3. Verb im Infinitive + **4.** -ed.

Signalwörter für diese Zeit sind **ago** *(früher)*, **yesterday** *(gestern)*, **in** + Jahreszahl *(im Jahre ...)*, **last night, month, year** *(letzte Nacht, letzten Monat, letztes Jahr)* oder **the other day** *(letztens)*.

Lesen Sie den Text noch einmal. Suchen Sie nach allen Formen im *simple past* und ergänzen Sie die Tabelle.

Regelmäßig		Unregelmäßig	
dared	used	was	led
stayed	asked	knew	began
whispered	lived	said	fell
looked	walked	saw	died
replied	shivered	went	

6. The White Lady

Mel erzählt ihrem Bruder von der weißen Frau. Hier ist ihre Geschichte in der Gegenwart. Wandeln Sie die Geschichte anschließend ins *simple past* um.

> Gwen and I walk to Castell Coch. We want to see the White Lady. People tell us that she is tall and thin and always wears a long white dress. She lives in the castle. We are really brave girls, but I feel scared because her ghost walks in the woods.

Gwen and I **1.** walked to Castell Coch. We **2.** wanted to see the White Lady. People **3.** told us that she was tall and thin and always **4.** worn a long white dress. She **5.** lived in the castle. We **6.** were really brave girls, but I **7.** felt scared because her ghost **8.** walked in the woods.

7. Die Steigerungsformen

Im Englischen erhalten ein- und zweisilbige Adjektive im Komparativ (also der 1. Steigerungsform) die Endung **-er**:

a soft cushion > a softer cushion *(ein weiches Kissen > weicheres ...)*

Den Superlativ (die 2. Steigerungsform) bildet man mit (the) + **-est**:

a soft cushion > the softest cushion *(das weichste Kissen)*

Viele zwei- und alle mehrsilbigen Adjektive werden mit Hilfe von **more** und (the) **most** gesteigert:

a beautiful dress > a more beautiful dress > the most beautiful dress
(ein schönes Kleid > ... schöneres ... > das schönste ...)

> Achtung: Bei der Steigerung wird **-y** zu **-ie**!
> Z. B.: **easy** > **easier** *(leicht, leichter)*

Vervollständigen Sie die Sätze mit der richtigen Steigerungsform des in Klammern angegebenen Adjektivs. Ein + steht dabei für die 1. Steigerungsform, ++ steht für den Superlativ.

1. Only bravest *(++ brave)* local teenagers dared to go to Castell Coch.
2. Mel was younger *(+ young)* and taller *(+ tall)* than Gwen.
3. The moon was paler *(+ pale)* and the sky was darked *(+ dark)* than the night before.
4. The trail grew thiner *(+ thin)* and thiner *(+ thin)*.
5. The white lady is thiner *(+ thin)* and taller *(+ tall)* than the girls.
6. The ghost wears more beautiful *(++ beautiful)* white dress.

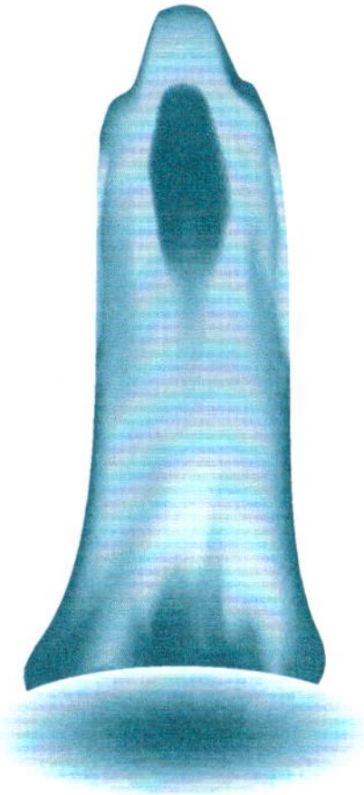

Aufgepasst bei folgenden Wörtern. Sie bilden nämlich eine Ausnahme, was ihre Steigerung angeht:

good - better - best	*(gut, besser, am besten)*
bad - worse - worst	*(schlecht, schlechter, am schlechtesten)*
much - more - most	*(viel, mehr, am meisten)*
little - less - least	*(wenig, weniger, am wenigsten)*
little - smaller - smallest	*(klein, kleiner, am kleinsten)*

Folgt Mel dem Rat Ihrer Freundin? Oder wartet der Geist etwa schon auf die beiden Mädchen...?

turret - *Turm*

sniffing - *schniefend*

to search - *(ab)suchen*

to lose sth. / sb. - *etw. / jdn. verlieren*

scream - *Schrei*

mud - *Schlamm*

dirt - *Dreck*

"No, look, you can see the top of the castle above the trees," replied Mel, pointing up at two dark **turrets**. "We're nearly there. All we have to do is touch the wall."

They continued to walk and soon the wall of the old castle was in front of them.

"See!" said Mel with a smile. "There was nothing to be afraid of!"

It was then, however, that they heard a strange noise behind them. It was a low, moaning, **sniffing** noise.

"What…what is that, Mel?" asked Gwen. "It sounds like someone crying."

Turning, they looked into the trees behind them, and there in the darkness they saw a figure in white moving in their direction.

"The White Lady!" Mel shouted. "Run!"

"Which way?" screamed Gwen, her torch **searching** the trees for another trail.

"This way!" said Mel, not waiting for her smaller friend.

"Wait!" cried Gwen, who could not run as fast.

For a moment she thought she had **lost** Mel, but then she heard a terrible **scream**.

"Mel, where are you?" Gwen said, searching the darkness with her torch.

"Help me! I'm here! I'm in the big hole! Get me out! Quick!"

Pointing her torch to the ground, Gwen saw her friend at the bottom of a big hole, her glasses on the floor next to her and **mud** and **dirt** in her hair.

"Okay, wait a second," said Gwen. "I think I can…"

But then she saw the **expression** on Mel's face change, and she heard the strange moaning sound.

"The White Lady!" Mel shouted. "Gwen, she's behind you!"

And Gwen, **terrified** now, slowly turned to look at the figure in white who was standing behind her.

"Mrs Williams?" she asked with surprise.

"Oh, hello Gwen, is that you? What are you doing **out here** in the middle of the night?" said an **elderly lady** in a white coat. Standing next to the elderly Mrs Williams was her Jack Russell Terrier, Davey, who was sniffing and moaning as he searched the long grass of the forest.

"Is it her?" Mel shouted from the hole. "Is it the White Lady?"

"Oh I see," said Mrs Williams quietly. "Looking for the ghost are you?"

Gwen **nodded**.

"Well," said the elderly lady with a smile. "When you tell the story to the other girls, make sure you tell them that I was **terrifying**." ■

expression - *Ausdruck*

terrified - *verängstigt*

out here - *hier draußen*

elderly lady - *ältere Dame*

to nod - *nicken*

terrifying - *furchteinflößend*

8. The Ghost

Haben Sie den Text aufmerksam gelesen? Beantworten Sie dann die folgenden Fragen.

1. All the girls have to do is...
- ❍ **A** talk to the White Lady.
- ❍ **B** touch the wall.
- ❍ **C** enter the Castell.

2. Who can run fast?
- ❍ **A** Mel
- ❍ **B** Gwen
- ❍ **C** the White Lady

3. What happens to Mel?
- ❍ **A** She falls into a hole.
- ❍ **B** She touches the wall.
- ❍ **C** She slips and falls down onto the ground.

4. Where do the girls meet the Lady?
- ❍ **A** She is behind Gwen.
- ❍ **B** She is in front of Gwen.
- ❍ **C** She is in the hole.

5. Who sniffs and moans?
- ❍ **A** the White Lady
- ❍ **B** Mel
- ❍ **C** Mrs Williams' dog

6. Who is the White Lady?
- ❍ **A** a dog
- ❍ **B** Mrs Williams
- ❍ **C** a ghost

Die Weiße Frau hat schon so manch einen in Angst und Schrecken versetzt. Man erzählt sich sogar, dass Lady Bute, die Witwe von Lord Bute, der die Burg im 19. Jahrhundert kaufte und renovierte, von ihr aus der Burg vertrieben wurde. Wenn man sich aber nicht vor Geistern fürchtet, wird man von Castell Coch begeistert sein. Die walisische Burganlage ist hervorragend erhalten und auch im Inneren hochinteressant.

9. Terr...

Im Text finden sich zwei Wörter, die ähnlich klingen und mit *terr-* beginnen. Finden Sie die Wörter und tragen Sie sie ein!

1. terrified

2. terrifying

Diese Wörter stammen vom lateinischen **terrere** ab, was so viel wie erschrecken bedeutet: **terribl** *(schrecklich)*, **terrifying** *(erschreckend, Angst einflößend)*, **terrified:** *erschrocken*. Aber, Achtung, dieses Wort ist positiv: **terrific** *(schrecklich toll)*.

Vervollständigen Sie jetzt den folgenden Text, den Mel ein paar Tage später erzählt, und setzen Sie die richtigen Wörter ein.

I felt really **3.** ____________ when I was in that hole. I was dirty and afraid. The sounds I heard were really **4.** ____________. In the end, all ended well. The ghost was no one else but Mrs Williams. So you know what, now I can tell you a great – no, wait – a **5.** ____________ story! What do you think?

10. Was Sie nicht sagen ...

Mel und Gwen unterhalten sich. Welche Wörter für „sagen“ verwenden sie? Tipp: Blättern Sie zum Anfang der Geschichte zurück. Ordnen Sie dann die Wörter ihrer Übersetzung zu.

1.	reply	**A**	rufen (laut)
2.	say	**B**	schreien
3.	ask	**C**	sagen
4.	shout	**D**	antworten
5.	scream	**E**	rufen (panisch)
6.	cry	**F**	fragen

“The White Lady!” Mel shouted. “Run!”

“Die Weiße Lady!” rief Mel laut. “Lauf!“

11. Past Progressive

Das **past progressive** ist eine Zeit, die es so im Deutschen nicht gibt.

Es wird gebildet mit **was** oder **were** + Verb + **ing:**

I was walking. You were walking. He was walking. etc.

Das **past progressive** beschreibt Handlungen in der Vergangenheit, die über eine längere Zeit hinweg passiert sind, oder die andauern, während etwas anderes beginnt oder gleichzeitig abläuft. Signalwörter sind **while** *(während)* oder **when** *(als)*.

Davey was sniffing and moaning while he searched the long grass.

Hier in diesem Satz treffen beide Zeiten aufeinander: Davey, der Hund, schnüffelt und stöhnt (= andauernde Handlung), während er das Gras durchsucht (= neue Handlung).

Entscheiden Sie nun selbst, welche Zeit die richtige ist:

Mel **1.** was hiking *(hike)* along the path when she suddenly **2.** heared *(hear)* a noise behind her. When she **3.** was turning *(turn)* around, she **4.** saw *(see)* a White Lady, who **5.** laughed *(laugh)*.

12. Possessive 's

Sehen Sie sich folgende Sätze an. Wie wird Besitz oder Zugehörigkeit ausgedrückt?

Mel has a torch. Mel's torch works fine. *...Mels Taschenlampe...*
Gwen and Mel have torches. The girls' torches both work fine.
...Die Taschenlampen der Mädchen...
The light of the torch is bright. *...Licht (von) der Taschenlampe...*

Bei einer Person wird Zugehörigkeit mit **1.** 's ausgedrückt.
Bei mehreren Personen wird Zugehörigkeit mit **2.** s' ausgedrückt.
Dinge bilden eine Ausnahme. Hier wird Zugehörigkeit mit **3.** of ausgedrückt.

Bilden Sie nun aus den vorgegebenen Wörtern Sätze mit der entsprechenden Bedeutung.

But then she saw the expression on Mel's face change, and she heard the strange moaning sound.

Aber dann sah sie, dass sich Mels Gesichtsausdruck veränderte, und sie hörte das seltsame, stöhnende Geräusch.

4. Mels Gesicht war blass. *(face / Mel / pale / to be)*
Mel's face was pale.

5. Die Wand des Schlosses war alt. *(castle / wall / the / to be / old)*
The wall of the castle was old.

6. Die Taschenlampen der Mädchen waren hell. *(the / girls / bright / torches / to be)*
~~The ... torches of the girls were bright.~~
The girls' torches were bright.

Übrigens: Bei Substantiven, die auf **-s** enden (z. B. bei vielen Namen oder bei Substantiven im Plural), steht nur ein Apostroph nach dem **-s: Mrs Williams' dog.** *Der Hund von Mrs Williams.*

4. A LITTLE SLICE OF HEAVEN

“This,” says Catherine Milligan, “is A LITTLE SLICE OF HEAVEN.”

She is standing on a small green hill in the middle of the Cotswolds. Below her is the famous village of Bibury, with its idyllic stone COTTAGES, GENTLE river Coln, and typical English church. Above her is a clear blue sky and a warm summer sun.

“Heaven,” she repeats, and A SMILE APPEARS on her face.

Now, for most PEOPLE a smile is A PERFECTLY NORMAL THING, but Catherine Milligan is not most people. No, Catherine Milligan is a very important business woman, and UNFORTUNATELY she does not have the time to smile.

In fact, for fifty-one weeks of every year, Catherine Milligan does not have time to do anything apart from work. For fifty-one weeks of every year, Catherine Milligan does not smile, she does not laugh, and she does not relax.

However, every year on the first of August, Catherine leaves her office in the centre of London. She turns off her mobile phone. She packs a small suitcase and she drives her red sports car north.

No one knows where Catherine goes because she never tells anyone. She never tells anyone, because for Catherine a real holiday is PEACE AND QUIET.

So, when Catherine does smile, she is normally alone and there is no one to see her do it.

a little slice of heaven – *ein kleines Stück Himmel*
cottage – *kleines Landhaus*
gentle – *hier: sanft*
a smile appears – *ein Lächeln erscheint*
people – *Menschen*
a perfectly normal thing – *etwas ganz normales*
unfortunately – *leider*
peace and quiet – *Ruhe und Frieden*

Today, however, she is not alone.

"Beautiful," a voice says, and Catherine SHRIEKS IN SURPRISE and turns to see a man sitting on a stone wall.

"Sorry," the man says with a smile. "I didn't mean TO SCARE you."

Catherine looks at him for a moment. He is a dark haired man with blue eyes and a handsome face.

"It's fine," says Catherine.

"No, I'm very sorry," he says again. "I'm very sorry, because now you're not smiling."

Catherine says nothing, but begins to walk back down the hill to the village.

to shriek in surprise - *vor Überraschung aufschreien*
to scare - *erschrecken*

1. THE FIRST ENCOUNTER

Haben Sie den Text aufmerksam gelesen? Beantworten Sie dann die folgenden Fragen. Mehrere Antworten können richtig sein.

1. What type of place is Bibury?

- ❍ **A** It's a very busy place.
- ❍ **B** It's a very famous place.
- ❍ **C** It's not a very nice place.

2. Why is Catherine here?

- ❍ **A** She's visiting friends.
- ❍ **B** She's here for a business meeting.
- ❍ **C** She's here on holiday.

3. Why does Catherine not tell anyone?

- ❍ **A** She wants to be alone.
- ❍ **B** She wants to surprise her family.
- ❍ **C** She ran away from home.

4. What is different today?

- ❍ **A** A man speaks to Catherine.
- ❍ **B** Nothing. Everything is just as always.
- ❍ **C** Catherine decided to join a group of visitors.

5. Why does the man talk to Catherine?

- ❍ **A** He wants to scare her.
- ❍ **B** He asks her for the way.
- ❍ **C** He just wants to be friendly.

6. How does Catherine react?

- ❍ **A** She is angry.
- ❍ **B** She is frightened.
- ❍ **C** She ignores him.

Catherine befindet sich im Herzen Englands. Diese wunderschöne hügelige Gegend ist seit dem Mittelalter sehr wohlhabend und ist oftmals der Ort, an dem sich wohlhabende Londoner zur Ruhe setzen. Im Osten liegt die Stadt Oxford und mehrere Flüsse durchziehen die Landschaft.

2. A SLICE OF HEAVEN

Catherine ist ganz begeistert von dieser wunderschönen Landschaft, die sie selbst als *slice of heaven* beschreibt. Aber was gehört dazu? Lesen Sie den Text noch einmal aufmerksam durch und ordnen Sie die Ausdrücke, die zusammengehören, jeweils den deutschen Übersetzungen zu.

stone • cottage • church • summer • river • hill • sun • sky •
warm • typical • gentle • small • blue • English • clear • green • idyllic

1. idyllic stone cottage ______ *(idyllisches Steinhäuschen)*
2. gentle river ______ *(sanft fließender Fluss)*
3. clear blue sky ______ *(klarer, blauer Himmel)*
4. warm summer sun ______ *(warme Sommersonne)*
5. typical English church ______ *(typisch englische Kirche)*
6. small green hill ______ *(kleiner grüner Hügel)*

Himmel wird im Englischen mit **heaven** oder **sky** übersetzt, aber die Begriffe sind nicht gleichbedeutend: **heaven** ist der religiöse Himmel, **sky** der Himmel, an dem man Sonne und Wolken findet.

3. BEING A BUSINESS PERSON

Catherine ist eine hart arbeitende Geschäftsfrau. Mit welchen Gegenständen und Eigenschaften kann man sie in Verbindung bringen?

1. The thing a business person uses to put his or her clothes in.

2. The place a business person works in.

3. The device a business person uses for contacting others.

4. Another word for having no time to relax.

5. A place you pay for and where you can sleep.

6. When you come together with people and discuss important things, it's called a … .

A busy

B meeting

C hotel room

D office

E small suitcase

F mobile phone

4. MÄNNER UND FRAUEN BESCHREIBEN

Um gut aussehende Personen zu beschreiben, gibt es viele Begriffe – aber nicht alle sind für Männer und Frauen gleichermaßen geeignet. Ordnen Sie zu, welche Wörter nur für Männer passen und welche nur für Frauen, sowie welche Begriffe man für beide Geschlechter verwenden darf.

pretty • good-looking • handsome • attractive • gorgeous

1. pretty
2. gorgeous
3. handsome
4. good-looking
5. attractive

Nur Männer können **handsome** sein. Bezeichnet man eine Frau als **handsome**, sagt man damit aus, dass sie sehr androgyn wirkt. Umgekehrt gilt es für **pretty**. Ein Mann, den man so bezeichnet, dem sagt man nach, er sei tuntig.

NO ONE KNOWS WHERE CATHERINE GOES BECAUSE SHE NEVER TELLS ANYONE.

Niemand weiß, wohin Catherine fährt, weil sie es niemandem erzählt.

5. SOME OR ANY

- **Some** verwendet man in bejahten Aussagesätzen, Bitten sowie Fragen, wenn man erwartet, dass die Antwort ja ist.
  Would you like some wine? *Hätten Sie / Hättest du gern (etwas) Wein?*
- **Any** verwendet man bei Fragen oder bei verneinten Aussagesätzen.
  Have you got any idea who that man is? - No, I haven't got any idea.
  Haben Sie / Hast du eine Ahnung, wer dieser Mann ist? – Nein.

Die beiden Wörter können dabei unterschiedliche Bedeutungen annehmen: *einige, etwas, ein paar, manche, keine, irgendeine* oder *irgendwelche* oder sogar unübersetzt bleiben.

Ähnlich ist es mit ihren Zusammensetzungen **someone – anyone, somebody – anybody, something – anything, sometime – anytime, somewhere – anywhere.**

Was sich Catherine wohl denkt, als der Mann sie anspricht? Vervollständigen Sie den Text mit den folgenden Wörtern.

somebody • something • anything • anywhere • sometime • anytime • any

Catherine thinks to herself: I haven't got **1.** ___any___ idea who that man is. I haven't seen him **2.** ___anywhere___ or **3.** ___anytime___ before. He must be a tourist, just like me. Maybe I will ask **4.** ___something___ later if they know him. There is **5.** ___something___ nice about him. I cannot find **6.** ___anything___ I don't like about him, just that I want to be left in peace and quiet. Maybe **7.** ___somebody___ soon, when I have relaxed a little, and I meet him again, then I'll talk to him.

Was will der Mann nur von Catherine? Wird sie ihn los, oder folgt er ihr gar am Ende und ruiniert ihren Urlaub?

"Are you walking back to Bibury?" the man says. "Me too." And before Catherine can say anything the man is walking next to her.

"Well, my name's Richard. Richard Parker," he says. "I'm here on holiday. It's a lovely place. Are you on holiday too? Are you here to HIKE? I love to hike."

to hike - *wandern*

Catherine says nothing, but the man does not seem to NOTICE.

to notice - *bemerken*

"Do you know the area? Is this your first time here? What do you like about the Cotswolds?"

Catherine stops walking and looks at the man DIRECTLY IN HIS EYES. "What do I like? I like the peace and quiet," she says, then she begins to walk more quickly down the hill.

directly in his eyes - *direkt in seine Augen*

For a moment the man is silent, then he smiles again. "The peace and quiet? Yes, me too. I like that too. I love the hills and the river. It's a very beautiful area. Are you staying in the village?"

Catherine says nothing, but she feels very annoyed now.

"There are some excellent walks here. I think the weather is going to be good for the week. You know, there's a nice pub in the village, they do excellent food... maybe one night..."

Catherine stops again and looks at the man. "Excuse me, but can you please stop talking to me? This is my holiday. I have one holiday every year and all I want is some peace and quiet. Do you understand?"

For a moment the man with the dark hair continues to smile, but then, slowly, he stops. "Oh, I see. I'm sorry...I...well, have a nice day."

to turn around *- sich umdrehen*
back up *- zurück nach oben*
to enjoy *- genießen*
suddenly *- plötzlich*
about this pub *- hier: wegen des Pubs*

Then the man TURNS AROUND and begins to walk slowly BACK UP the hill.

Good, thinks Catherine, and she turns and continues to walk down the hill.

"What a strange man," she says. "A very happy person. Very friendly, too. And he does have a nice smile."

Catherine stops and looks at the beautiful view in front of her: the idyllic stone cottages, the gentle river, the small green hills. "A little slice of heaven," she says again, but this time she does not smile. "A little slice of heaven…but no one to ENJOY it with."

SUDDENLY, without thinking, Catherine Milligan turns around and begins to run up the hill.

"Wait!" she shouts, but she cannot see the strange, friendly man and she stops running.

"So…" says a voice, and Catherine shrieks in surprise again. "ABOUT THIS PUB… the food really is excellent."

And for the second time in fifty-two weeks… Catherine Milligan smiles. ■

6. RIGHT OR WRONG

Haben Sie den Text aufmerksam gelesen? Entscheiden Sie dann, ob folgende Aussagen richtig oder falsch sind.

	RIGHT	WRONG
1. Richard Parker lives in the Cotswolds.	❍	❍
2. The weather is going to be bad for the week.	❍	❍
3. Catherine doesn't want to talk to him at first.	❍	❍
4. The man says goodbye and walks slowly back up the hill.	❍	❍
5. Catherine suddenly no longer wants to be alone.	❍	❍

7. TALKING ABOUT HOLIDAY

Im Text tauchen viele Fragen auf, die man als Aufhänger für ein Urlaubsgespräch verwenden kann. Ordnen Sie den Fragen die passende Antwort zu:

1. Are you on holiday?
2. Are you here to hike?
3. Do you know the area?
4. What do you like about the place?
5. Are you staying in the village?

A It's very beautiful and has excellent pubs.
B Yes, I know it very well.
C Yes, I am. I'm staying in a small hotel.
D Yes, I am. I'm here for the week.
E No, I'm here to relax.

8. BESCHREIBUNGEN – SO WIRD'S LEBENDIGER

Catherine schildert ihrer besten Freundin wie ihr der Urlaub gefällt. Ordnen Sie die Begriffe ihrer deutschen Bedeutung zu und entziffern Sie dann, was Catherine schreibt. Leider sind bei vielen Wörtern die Buchstaben durcheinander gekommen.

1. lovely	**A** schnell
2. quickly	**B** hübsch
3. quiet	**C** glücklich
4. beautiful	**D** freundlich
5. annoyed	**E** ruhig
6. excellent	**F** wunderschön
7. nice	**G** genervt
8. strange	**H** nett
9. happy	**I** seltsam
10. friendly	**J** hervorragend

Dear Sue, I am so **11.** ____________ *(pypah)* to be here. The first days have passed so **12.** ____________ *(ckiquly)*. Everything here is so **13.** ____________ *(uteqi)* and **14.** ____________ *(autibeluf)*. I live in a **15.** ____________ *(olevyl)* small hotel with **16.** ____________ *(tnellecxe)* food and very **17.** ____________ *(einyldfr)* people. And I met a very **18.** ____________ *(icen)* young man. At first, however, I was a little **19.** ____________ *(oynaned)*, because I found it **20.** ____________ *(eganrst)* that he talked to me when I wanted to be left alone.

9. IM PUB

Diese Dinge finden Sie in einem *Pub*. Ordnen Sie die Bilder den Begriffen zu.

1

2

3

4

5

6

___ **A** bar

___ **B** bartender

___ **C** beer

___ **D** excellent food

___ **E** good music

___ **F** wine

In einem englischen Pub haben Sie beim Bier vier verschiedene Varianten zur Auswahl: **Ale**, **Lager**, **Porter** und **Stout**. **Ale** ist relativ bitter und **Lager** ist eher ein Helles oder Pils. **Porter** ist dunkles, malziges Bier und **Stout** ist besonders kräftiges **Porter**. In der Regel bestellen Sie im Pub allerdings kein Bier **(beer)**, sondern **(half) a pint of** + Name des Bieres oder der Sorte.
Na dann Prost oder wie die Engländer sagen: **Cheers!**

10. SICH ENTSCHULDIGEN

Das Eis zwischen den beiden ist endlich gebrochen. Im Text finden sich einige Ausdrücke, mit denen sich Catherine bei Richard für ihr anfänglich abweisendes Verhalten entschuldigen könnte. Lesen Sie nach, welche das sein könnten.

1. S____________________.

2. I'm ____________________.

3. E____________________.

Excuse me verwendet man, bevor etwas passiert, z. B. **Excuse me, can you help me, please?** *Entschuldigung, können Sie mir helfen?* **Sorry** sagt man, nachdem etwas passiert ist, z. B. **I'm very sorry that I ruined your holiday.** *Es tut mir sehr leid, dass ich Ihre Ferien verdorben habe.* Man kann es aber auch bei Bitten verwenden: **Sorry, can you tell your kid to stop kicking me?** *Entschuldigung, können Sie Ihrem Kind sagen, dass es aufhören soll mich zu treten?*

11. HOW TO PLACE AN ORDER

Catherine und Richard wollen in der Kneipe ein Bier bestellen. Bringen Sie den Dialog mit dem Kellner in die richtige Reihenfolge.

1. Thanks for your order. Food will be ready in a minute.
2. Hello, a pint of lager, please.
3. Yes, a sandwich with ham and cheese would be nice.
4. Anything else I can get you?
5. Hello, what can I do for you?

Richtige Reihenfolge: 5, 2, 4, 3, 1

5. The Banshee

For a long time, the old road that ran beside the bank of Strangford Lough was silent and empty.

It was *nearly midnight*, and now there were no cars travelling between the small towns of Comber and Whiterock on the eastern coast of Northern Ireland.

Occasionally, you could hear the sound of Irish folk music coming from the small country pub at Whiterock, but apart from that there was no sign of life by the water of the *lough*.

Then, a figure *appeared* on the road. It was the figure of a handsome young man with red hair and dark brown eyes. He was wearing a *smart* black shirt, grey trousers and black shoes. And it was because of these formal clothes that it seemed very strange that the man was running so quickly along the silent road.

"Stupid!" he said *to himself* as he ran. "You stupid, stupid man! How did you forget the date?

The twenty-ninth of February! It's the twenty-ninth of February today!"

He was *breathing* very quickly, and there was sweat on his face. When he saw a road sign at the side of the road he stopped and looked in both directions.

"Only a mile to Whiterock," he said, but his face was worried and unhappy. "Only a mile, but she knows where I'm going! She might be *right behind me*!" And he turned to look back along the road to the *distant lights* of Comber.

nearly midnight – *fast Mitternacht*

occasionally – *gelegentlich*

lough – *Irisch: See*

to appear – *auftauchen*

smart – *schick*

to himself – *zu sich selbst*

to breathe – *atmen*

right behind me – *direkt hinter mir*

distant lights – *ferne Lichter*

darkness – *Dunkelheit*

He could see nothing in the *darkness*, but more importantly he could hear nothing.

"Come on, Dylan! You need to think! She knows you want to go to Whiterock. She knows you want a nice, cold pint of Guinness. So where can you go *instead*?"

instead – *stattdessen*
squealing sound – *schrilles Geräusch*
banshee – *Todesfee*
terrified – *verängstigt*
silhouette – *Silhouette*

And then he heard it. A high *squealing sound* like some sort of terrible creature. Like some sort of terrible *banshee*.

"No!" he shouted, his face suddenly *terrified*. "It's only ten to midnight. Ten minutes! I need to hide for ten minutes!"

He looked to the left and saw the *silhouette* of Sketrick Island on the dark water of the lough.

"The bridge!" he shouted. "If I can get to the bridge…"

to look over one's shoulder – *über die Schulter schauen*

He began to run again, this time faster than before. While he ran he occasionally *looked over his shoulder*, and soon he saw bright white lights in the distance.

In front of him the road turned left and he could see the thin bridge that led to the island; but it was too far away.

to shriek – *kreischen*

"Dylan!" a voice *shrieked* from behind him, and he heard the terrible sound of laughter in the darkness.

muddy – *schlammig*

Suddenly, without thinking, he jumped over the low wall to his left and fell into a *muddy* field.

to sink into – *in etw. einsinken*

Then he was running again, his smart black shoes *sinking into* the mud. ▶▷▶

1. On the Bank of Strangford Lough

Haben Sie den Text aufmerksam gelesen? Beantworten Sie dann die folgenden Fragen. Mehrere Antworten können richtig sein.

1. Why is the old road silent and empty?
- ❍ **A** Everyone is on holiday.
- ❍ **B** It's very late.
- ❍ **C** It's very early in the morning.

2. What is Dylan wearing?
- ❍ **A** A pair of jeans and a T-shirt.
- ❍ **B** Sports clothes.
- ❍ **C** A shirt and grey trousers.

3. Why does Dylan not reach the bridge?
- ❍ **A** It's too far away.
- ❍ **B** His car broke down.
- ❍ **C** He doesn't want to go there.

4. How does Dylan move?
- ❍ **A** He swims.
- ❍ **B** He runs.
- ❍ **C** He walks.

5. What sound does Dylan hear?
- ❍ **A** The mooing of cows.
- ❍ **B** The wind.
- ❍ **C** A squealing sound.

6. What does Dylan want to do in Whiterock?
- ❍ **A** Go to a pub.
- ❍ **B** Find a hotel.
- ❍ **C** Take the next train home.

2. *On the road*

For a long time, the old road that ran beside the bank of Strangford Lough was silent and empty.

Lange Zeit war es auf der Straße, die entlang des Ufers von Strangford Lough verlief, still und leer.

Dylan ist unterwegs. Im Text finden sich viele Wörter, die seinen Weg beschreiben. Ordnen Sie die Beschreibungen den Bildern zu.

1

2

3

4

5

6

___ **A** road sign

___ **B** old road

___ **C** island

___ **D** low wall

___ **E** bridge

___ **F** small town

3. Tageszeiten

Anders als in Deutschland wird die Uhrzeit in Großbritannien nicht im 24-Stunden-Rhythmus angegeben, sondern in **a.m.** und **p.m.** Die Abkürzung **a.m.** steht für **ante meridiem** und bedeutet Vormittag, **p.m.** für **post meridiem** und bedeutet Nachmittag. **Noon** bedeutet 12 Uhr Mittag, **midnight** bedeutet Mitternacht.

It was nearly midnight, and now there were no cars travelling between the small towns of Comber and Whiterock on the Eastern Coast of Northern Ireland.

Es war kurz vor Mitternacht. Im Moment fuhr kein Auto zwischen den kleinen Städten Comber und Whiterock an der Ostküste von Nordirland.

Ordnen Sie die folgenden Uhrzeiten und Tageszeiten in der richtigen Reihenfolge. Die früheste Zeit kommt zuerst. Wenn Tageszeit und Uhrzeit zusammenpassen, sortieren Sie entsprechend, z. B. ***noon (12 a.m.).***

noon • 1 a.m. • 5 p.m. • midnight • morning • afternoon • night • 7 p.m. • evening • 7 a.m. • 11 p.m. • 10 a.m. • 12 p.m.

Richtige Reihenfolge: ______________________________

____

____

4. Die Uhr

Wie war das nochmal mit der Uhr...? Aufgepasst! Auf Deutsch heißt es *halb zehn*, auf Englisch **half past nine**. Es geht also immer von der vollen Stunde weg. *Nach* heißt **past** und *vor* heißt **to**. *10 Minuten vor fünf* heißt dann **ten to five**.

... o'clock

a quarter past...

half past...

a quarter to...

Schreiben Sie nun die folgenden Uhrzeiten in Worten:

1. 8:00 p.m. 8 o'clock

2. 11:30 a.m. half past eleven

3. 3:45 a.m. a quater past three

4. 7:50 p.m. ten to 8 o'clock

5. 9:15 p.m. a quarter past nice

6. 4:05 a.m. five past four

5. Das Datum

Dylan hat sich ausgerechnet den 29. Februar ausgesucht. Aber wie macht man eigentlich Datumsangaben im Englischen?

Aufgepasst! In den USA wird das Datum anders geschrieben als in Großbritannien. Dort schreibt man zuerst den Monat und dann den Tag: **02/29/16** (entspricht dem 29. Februar 2016). In Großbritannien steht wie in Deutschland der Tag zuerst: **29/02/16** bzw. **29 February, 2016**.

Sie schreiben Briefe in die USA und nach Großbritannien. Wie sieht jeweils die korrekte Datumsangabe aus?

	USA	**GB**
1. Mai 2017	05/01/2017	01/05/17
26. August 2018	08/26/18	26/08/18
5. März 2020	03/05/20	05/03/20

Ihr Freund aus den USA kommt zu Besuch. Er hat sich für folgendes Datum angemeldet: 11/8/2017. Wann kommt er?

Lösung: 8/11/2017

6. Die Ordnungszahlen und das Datum

Wie war das nochmal, wenn man das Datum nicht nur schreiben, sondern sagen will? Es ist gar nicht schwer, wenn man die Ordnungszahlen parat hat.

1 > 1st, **first**	2 > 2nd, **second**	3 > 3rd, **third**	4 > 4th, **fourth**	5 > 5th, **fifth**
6 > 6th, **sixth**	7 > 7th, **seventh**	8 > 8th, **eighth**	9 > 9th, **ninth**	... ab jetzt muss man an die Zahl nur noch **-th** anhängen.

Endet die Zahl auf **-y**, wird das **-y** durch **-ieth** ersetzt:
20, twenty > 20th, twentieth
Beim Datum sagt man dann z. B. **May (the) fifth** oder **the fifth of May.**

Schreiben Sie jetzt das angezeigte Datum so, wie Sie es vorlesen würden.

1

the fifth of January

2

the twenty fourth of december

3

the 14th February

7. Warum denn nicht Meter?

Wie weit war es bis Whiterock? Lesen Sie nach und finden Sie heraus, welche Distanzangabe Dylan hier verwendet.

Lösung: ______________________________

Aber wie weit ist das denn in Meter? Überhaupt verwendet man in Großbritannien meist andere Längenangaben als in Deutschland. Finden Sie heraus, welche zusammenpassen?

1. mile — **A** 0,9 m

2. inch — **B** 1,6 km

3. yard — **C** 2,54 cm

4. foot / feet — **D** 30 cm

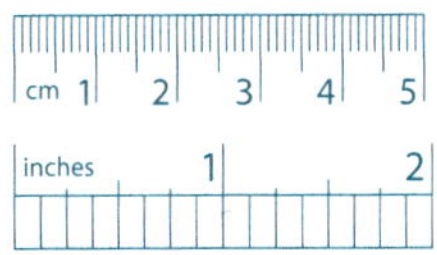

Wie weit sind folgende Strecken?

5. 5,4 miles ______________________________

6. 5,4 feet ______________________________

7. 7 yards ______________________________

8. 12 inches ______________________________

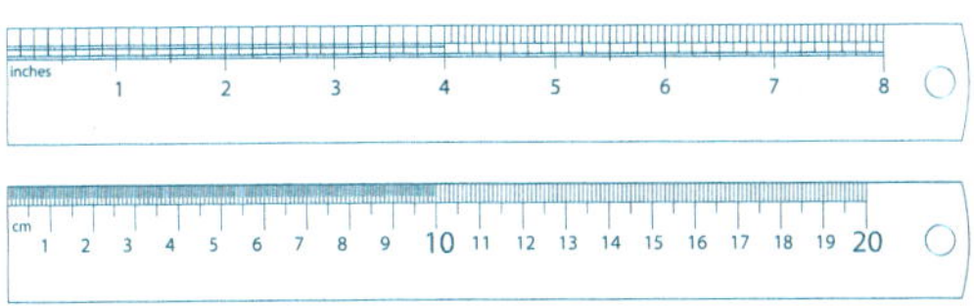

Dylan ist verständlicherweise in Panik. Wenn er nur wüsste, was die Todesfee von ihm will…

But where was he going to go? Behind him he could hear laughter and the high, squealing sound. In front of him was the dark water of Strangford Lough.

The water? But it was so cold at this time of year. He couldn't swim in it…

"But maybe there's a boat!" he said to himself, and he ran to the *shore* and began to search.

shore - *Ufer*

Behind him the high squealing sound stopped, but he knew that she was *still there*.

still there - *noch immer dort*

"Dylan?" the voice called in the darkness. "Where are you, Dylan?"

Then he saw it. A small and very old *rowing boat* at the edge of the water.

rowing boat - *Ruderboot*

"You'll never catch me!" he shouted, then ran to the small boat, pushed it into the water and *jumped into* it.

to jump into - *hineinspringen*

For a moment he was so happy that he wanted to laugh, but then, suddenly, he felt the boat move in the wrong direction.

And he heard the laughter in the darkness. "Oh, Dylan. Did you forget to *untie* the boat?" the voice said, and slowly the boat began to return to the shore.

to untie - *losmachen*

"*Stay away from me* you…you…banshee!" Dylan shouted when he saw the figure of the woman standing next to the water.

stay away from me - *bleib weg von mir*

She was a beautiful woman with long dark hair, green eyes, and a *mischievous* smile. "First *you make me chase you* on my old moped, then you call me a banshee. You're not a very nice boyfriend."

mischievous - *verschmitzt*

to make s.o. chase s.o. - *jdn. dazu bringen jdn. zu jagen*

Dylan shook his head. "I forgot. I forgot that it was a *leap year*. I forgot it was the twenty-ninth of February," he said, a small smile appearing on his face.

leap year - *Schaltjahr*

"So you *ran away*? Because you know that on the twenty-ninth of February, in Ireland, women ask men to marry them?"

to run away - *wegrennen*

"Yes," Dylan said from the boat.

And the woman smiled again. "Well, *guess* what my next question is..."

to guess - *raten*

8. *Was ist passiert?*

Das ist ja noch mal gut gegangen. Wiederholen Sie nun, was in der Geschichte passiert ist.
Bringen Sie die folgenden Sätze in die richtige Reihenfolge:

1. The woman wanted to ask Dylan an important question.
2. The boat began to return to the shore.
3. He jumped into a small rowing boat.
4. Dylan talked to the woman.
5. Dylan searched for a boat at the shore.
6. A beautiful woman was standing next to the water.

Richtige Reihenfolge: ______________________

Eine **Banshee** ist in der keltischen Mythologie ein weiblicher Geist der den Tod einer Person ankündigt. Sie ist vor allem für ihr Klagen und ihre Schreie berühmt, man hört sie eher als dass man sie sieht.

9. Am Wasser

Wollen Sie auch einen kleinen Bootsausflug machen? Ordnen Sie den Bildern die passenden Begriffe zu.

1

2

3

4

5

6

2 **A** rowing boat

3 **B** untie the knot

1 **C** to swim

__ **D** oar

__ **F** lough

__ **E** shore

Lough (Irisch für See) wird in Schottland **Loch** geschrieben und ist nicht zuletzt durch das Monster von Loch Ness bekannt. Die Ureinwohner der zwei Inseln Großbritannien und Irland waren Kelten. Diese beiden keltischen Wörter für See blieben in Irland und Schottland erhalten, aber nicht in England, wo sich durch die angelsächsische Besiedelung das Wort **lake** durchgesetzt hat.

10. Präpositionen

Dylans Flucht vor der Todesfee wird mit verschiedenen Präpositionen (Ortsangaben) beschrieben. Welche Begriffe entsprechen welcher Bedeutung?

1.	in front of	**A**	unter
2.	behind	**B**	neben
3.	next to	**C**	vor
4.	under	**D**	auf
5.	on	**E**	hinter

In front of him was the dark water of Strangford Lough.

Vor ihm lag das dunkle Gewässer von Strangford Lough.

11. Gegensätze ziehen sich an

Gegensätze ziehen sich an, heißt es. Finden Sie auch hier die passenden Gegenteile?

1.	dark	**A**	tall
2.	small	**B**	fast
3.	slow	**C**	light
4.	high	**D**	mischievous
5.	nice	**E**	low

12. Ort vor Zeit

Suddenly (...) he fell into a muddy field.

Plötzlich (...) fiel er in ein schlammiges Feld.

Im Englischen steht die Ortsangabe normalerweise vor der Zeitangabe, außer man setzt eine davon (zur Betonung) an den Satzanfang. Dann wird diese meist mit einem Komma abgetrennt. Bringen Sie die Satzteile in die richtige Reihenfolge.

1. Dylan | was near | before midnight | shortly | Whiterock.

____

____

2. wanted to hide | that day | until midnight | he | on Sketrick Island

____

____

3. women | in Ireland | to marry | men | ask | every year | them | on that very day.

____

____

Dylans Geschichte ist erfunden. Was es aber tatsächlich gibt, ist die Tradition des **leap day**. Alle vier Jahre am 29. Februar dürfen die Frauen ihren Geliebten einen Heiratsantrag machen, der nicht abgelehnt werden darf. Diese Tradition geht auf das 13. Jahrhundert zurück und wurde durch Königin Margaret von Schottland eingeführt. Wenn sich ein Mann weigerte, den Antrag anzunehmen, musste er eine Geldstrafe zahlen, die sich an seinem Besitz orientierte. Hoffen wir also, dass Dylan den Antrag annimmt...

6. The Next Step

It was, in Gerald's opinion, a perfect day. The sky was blue, the sun was high and there was a cool breeze coming from the north.

opinion - *Meinung*

Also, the location was fantastic. Bolton Abbey, in the heart of the Yorkshire Dales, was one of the most picturesque places in Britain, because the old Abbey was next to a gentle river in a green and beautiful valley.

picturesque - *malerisch*

Yes, perfect, he thought.

So why did he look so unhappy?

He was sitting on a picnic blanket by the river, the ruins of the old Abbey behind him. Sitting opposite him was his girlfriend Emma, and on the picnic blanket there was a selection of sandwiches, some summer fruit, and a bottle of champagne.

picnic blanket - *Picknickdecke*

"Are you okay, Gerald?" asked Emma. "You seem very quiet," she said as she finished her second cucumber sandwich.

quiet - *ruhig, still*

cucumber - *Gurke*

"What? Me? No, I'm fine. Perfect. It's a perfect day. A perfect location. A perfect picnic," he said.

However, it was obvious that Gerald was not fine. He was usually very talkative and cheerful, but today he was silent and nervous. A perfect picnic," he said. "Nervous, me? No, I'm perfect, it's a perfect day," he said, again putting his hand into his pocket and touching the small black box.

obvious - *offensichtlich*

talkative - *gesprächig*

to touch - *anfassen, berühren*

1. A perfect day

Haben Sie den Text aufmerksam gelesen? Beantworten Sie dann die folgenden Fragen. Mehrere Antworten können richtig sein.

1. Why was it a perfect day?
- ❍ **A** The weather was nice.
- ❍ **B** The place was perfect.
- ❍ **C** The restaurant was very good.

2. Who is Emma?
- ❍ **A** Gerald's wife.
- ❍ **B** Gerald's sister.
- ❍ **C** Gerald's girlfriend.

3. Gerald is...
- ❍ **A** happy.
- ❍ **B** nervous.
- ❍ **C** quiet.

4. They are having a picnic with...
- ❍ **A** sandwiches.
- ❍ **B** wine.
- ❍ **C** fruit.

5. What does Emma eat?
- ❍ **A** a bacon sandwich.
- ❍ **B** a cucumber sandwich.
- ❍ **C** an egg sandwich.

6. What does Gerald touch?
- ❍ **A** Emma's hand.
- ❍ **B** the bottle of champagne.
- ❍ **C** a small black box.

Erfunden wurde das **Sandwich** übrigens von einem Briten – nämlich von John Montagu, dem 4. Earl of Sandwich, einer Kleinstadt in der Grafschaft Kent. Als begeisterter Kartenspieler fand er immer keine Zeit, um in Ruhe zu essen. Stattdessen ließ er sich sein Essen (meistens Rindfleisch) zwischen 2 Brotscheiben bringen, und konnte so gleichzeitig essen und spielen. Seine Freunde fanden das so kurios, dass sie diese Art des Brotes kurzerhand nach ihm benannten. Das **Sandwich** war geboren.

2. Eigenschaften

In der Geschichte geht es viel um Geralds Gemütszustand. Finden Sie im Text die englischen Adjektive, die zu diesen deutschen Übersetzungen passen.

However,
it was obvious
that Gerald was
not fine.

Aber es war offensichtlich,
dass Gerald sich nicht
wohl fühlte.

positive Eigenschaften

1. glücklich ______________

2. gut ______________

3. gesprächig ______________

4. fröhlich ______________

negative Eigenschaften

5. unglücklich ______________

6. nicht gut ______________

7. ruhig ______________

8. nervös ______________

Wie ist Geralds Stimmung im Augenblick?

Gerald is **9.** ______________.

He is **10.** ______________ and **11.** ______________.

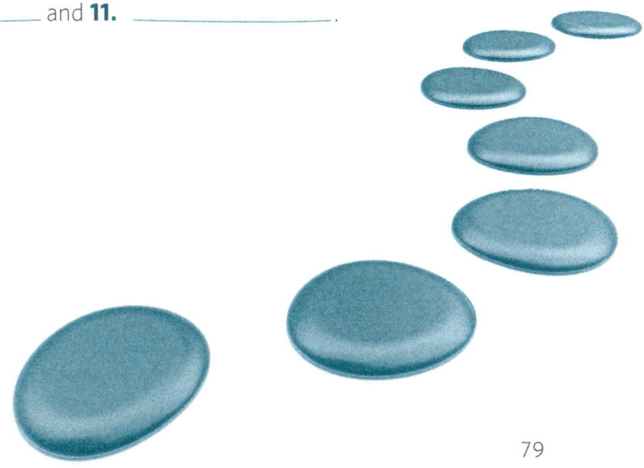

The sky was blue,
the sun was high and
there was a cool breeze
coming from the north.

Der Himmel war blau, die Sonne stand hoch oben und eine kühle Brise wehte von Norden.

3. The weather

Let's talk about the weather. Ein allseits beliebtes Thema für den Smalltalk: das Wetter. Gerald und Emma hatten das perfekte Wetter für ein Picknick, doch es ist bekanntlich nicht immer so in England. Wiederholen Sie hier einige Wörter zum Thema Wetter, indem Sie den Bildern die entsprechenden Sätze zuordnen.

1

2

3

4

5

6

___ **A** The weather is fine.

___ **B** It is very sunny and hot.

___ **C** It is cloudy.

___ **D** It is very cold and rainy.

___ **E** It is very foggy.

___ **F** It is snowing.

Und wenn es richtig schüttet, dann fielen früher sprichwörtlich sogar Katzen und Hunde vom Himmel: **It's raining cats and dogs.** *Es schüttet wie aus Eimern.* Leider ist dieses schöne Sprichwort mittlerweile veraltet. Heute sagt man: **It's pouring down (with rain).** *Es gießt in Strömen.*

4. The landscape

Berühmt ist England für seine wunderschöne Landschaft. Kein Wunder, dass Emma und Gerald Bolton Abbey ausgewählt haben. Kennen Sie noch mehr Begriffe, die mit Landschaft zu tun haben? Ordnen Sie zu:

1

2

3

4

5

6

___ **A** valley

___ **B** forest

___ **C** mountain

___ **D** waterfall

___ **E** river

___ **F** coast

Vielleicht ahnen Sie schon, warum Gerald so nervös ist und was es mit der kleinen schwarzen Schachtel in seiner Hose auf sich hat...

But Gerald was not perfect, in fact he was incredibly nervous. He was incredibly nervous, because today was the day he was going to propose to Emma.

"More champagne?" he said, pouring Emma another large glass and trying to smile.

"Er, okay," she said, "but are you sure there's nothing you want to talk about?"

For a moment Gerald hesitated, then he looked around for some distraction.

"Oh look, Emma, stepping stones!"

He pointed to a line of stones which crossed the gentle river, and the small group of children who were jumping from stone to stone and laughing.

Emma smiled. "Oh yes, that does look fun. Should we have a go?"

Gerald said nothing for a few seconds. Instead, he imagined how romantic it would be to ask Emma to marry him while they were in the middle of the river on the stepping stones.

Perfect! He thought.

"Yes, I think we should," he said calmly. "Come on, let's go!"

They stood up together and began to slowly walk towards the edge of the river and the grey stones that crossed it.

"Oh, actually, it looks a little more difficult than I thought," said Emma.

incredibly - *unglaublich*
to propose to s.b. - *jdm. einen Heiratsantrag machen*
to pour - *einschenken*
to hesitate - *zögern*
distraction - *Ablenkung*
stepping stones - *Trittsteine*
to have a go - *etw. versuchen*
calmly - *ruhig*
edge - *Rand*
actually - *tatsächlich*

However, Gerald did not hear this, because he was once more checking that the small black box was still in his shorts pocket.

"You go first," he said to Emma.

"Okay," she said, carefully stepping onto the first stone. ▶▷▶

5. In the middle of the river

Gerald ist unglaublich nervös. Warum? Haben Sie den zweiten Teil der Geschichte verstanden? Kreuzen Sie an, ob folgende Aussagen richtig oder falsch sind.

		RIGHT	WRONG
1.	Emma thinks Gerald is fine.	❍	❍
2.	Gerald wants to marry Emma.	❍	❍
3.	Some children are playing football at the river.	❍	❍
4.	Gerald thinks it is romantic to ask Emma to marry him in the middle of the river.	❍	❍
5.	It is very easy to cross the river on the grey stones.	❍	❍

6. Go, go, go

Bei vielen Aufforderungen im Englischen wird das Wort *go* verwendet. Lesen Sie noch einmal nach und finden Sie die drei Ausdrücke im Text:

1. ______________________ *(Probier es!)*

2. ______________________ *(Los geht's!)*

3. ______________________ *(Du zuerst!)*

Viele Jahre später erinnern sich Emma und Gerald an diese Szene. Füllen Sie die Lücken und setzen Sie die drei Aufforderungen richtig ein. Achtung, im letzten Fall muss die Wendung angepasst werden (an die Person und die Zeit).

Emma: "Do you remember the day we went to Bolton Abbey? It was a beautiful day and we wanted to cross that river. It looked fun, so we wanted to **4.** ________________. You told me 'come on,' **5.** ________________. So I did. I **6.** ________________."

7. Kleine Wörter

In der Szene werden viele unterschiedliche kleine Wörter oder Redewendungen verwendet, die die Gespräche lebendig machen. Ordnen Sie diese ihrer Übersetzung zu.

1. for a moment	**A** stattdessen
2. instead	**B** eigentlich
3. actually	**C** aber
4. however	**D** einen Augenblick lang

Gerald erinnert sich natürlich an den Tag. Vervollständigen Sie seine Erzählung und setzen Sie dabei die Wörter aus der Übung oben sinnvoll ein.

Gerald: "Of course I remember that day. **5.** ________________, I had planned to propose to you when we drank the champagne. **6.** ________________, I was too nervous. **7.** ________________, I suggested to go across those stepping stones. When you said yes, I thought **8.** ________________ that proposing to you on the stepping stones would be even more romantic."

He was incredibly nervous, because today was the day he was going to propose to Emma.

Er war unglaublich nervös, denn heute war der Tag, an dem er Emma einen Heiratsantrag machen würde.

8. Going to-Future

Da hat Gerald ja was vor! Da er den festen Plan gefasst hat, um Emmas Hand anzuhalten, wird die Zeitform des **going to-future** verwendet. Es wird wie folgt gebildet:

to be (am / is / are) + going to + Infinitiv

I am		*Ich werde*	
You are	**going to propose.**	*Du wirst*	*einen Antrag machen.*
He is		*Er wird*	

Die übliche Zeitform zum Wiedergeben von Geschichten und Erzählungen ist das **past tense**. Da Geralds Plan, Emma einen Antrag zu machen, in der Vergangenheit gefasst wurde, erscheint das **going to-future** hier in der Geschichte mit einer Form von **to be** im **past tense**. Befinden wir uns in der Gegenwart und sprechen über Pläne für die Zukunft, verwenden wir eine Form von **to be** im **present tense**.

Jetzt sind Sie dran! Übertragen Sie folgende Sätze aus dem *present tense* ins *going to-future*.

1. Gerald pours Emma another large glass of champagne.

____

2. Gerald says nothing for a few seconds.

____

3. Gerald checks that the small box is still in his shorts pocket.

____

Ob dieser Heiratsantrag mitten auf dem Fluss wohl so romantisch wird, wie Gerald sich das vorstellt?

to cross - *überqueren*
to have to - *müssen*
to reach - *erreichen*
to slip - *ausrutschen*
to wobble - *wackeln*
to regain - *wiedererlangen*
balance - *Gleichgewicht*
be careful - *sei vorsichtig*
huge - *hier: breit*
to struggle - *sich abmühen*

Slowly, they began to cross the river, and Gerald was happy to see that Emma was smiling and laughing.

Yes, this was certainly the perfect time. Now, he just had to think about how to ask her the big question.

"Emma," he said, while carefully following her across the large stones. "Actually, I do have something to speak to you about."

"Oh, really?" she asked, as she reached the middle of the river.

"Yes, I wanted to speak to you about, well, about our future, about us. Do you understand?"

"Er, I don't really..." she began to say, but before she could finish her foot slipped on a wet stone. For a moment she wobbled, but then regained her balance. Laughing, she moved to the next stone and turned round to warn Gerald. "Gerald, that next step..."

"The next step! Exactly!" Gerald said, not understanding. "Yes, I want to talk to you about the next step, and I want to ask you..."

"No, Gerald. Be careful!" Emma shouted.

But Gerald was concentrating on the small black box which he was taking from his pocket. He stepped onto the wet stone, slipped, then fell with a scream of surprise into the cold water of the river.

He was so surprised, in fact, that he threw the small black box up into the air and it landed directly in Emma's hands.

"Gerald? What's this?" said Emma as she opened the box, a huge smile appearing on her face.

"It's..." he said, struggling to stand, a smile appearing on his own face. "The next step?"

9. The proposal

Nun, das war zumindest ein ungewöhnlicher Antrag... Bringen Sie die folgenden Sätze in die richtige Reihenfolge:

A Emma's foot slipped on a wet stone.

B Gerald threw the small black box into Emma's hands.

C Gerald proposed to Emma.

D Gerald and Emma began to cross the river.

E Gerald fell into the cold water.

F Emma warned Gerald of the next step.

Richtige Reihenfolge: ______________________

Wenn es dann so weit ist, dass Emma und Gerald heiraten, gilt für die Kleidung der Braut folgende Regel: **Something old, something new, something borrowed, something blue and a lucky six-pence in your shoe.** Das heißt, sie braucht *etwas Altes, etwa Neues, etwas Geliehenes, etwas Blaues, und muss einen Glückspfennig in ihren Schuh legen.*

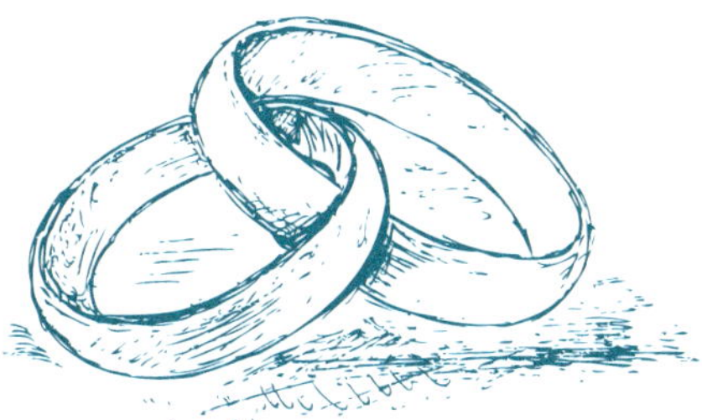

10. Immer in Bewegung

Gerald und Emma sind sehr geschickt darin, über die Steine zu klettern. Schauen wir uns einmal an, welche Verben wir im Text finden, die mit Bewegung zu tun haben. Finden Sie jeweils die passende Übersetzung:

1. to cross	___	**A**	treten
2. to follow	___	**B**	fallen
3. to reach	___	**C**	folgen
4. to slip	___	**D**	landen
5. to wobble	___	**E**	sich bewegen
6. to move	___	**F**	erreichen
7. to turn around	___	**G**	ausrutschen
8. to step	___	**H**	überqueren
9. to fall	___	**I**	werfen
10. to throw	___	**J**	sich umdrehen
11. to land	___	**K**	wackeln, schwanken

"Emma," he said, while carefully following her across the large stones.

„Emma," sagte er, während er ihr vorsichtig über die großen Steine hinweg folgte.

11. Das Adverb

...and it landed directly in Emma's hands.

...und sie landete direkt in Emmas Händen.

Adjektive beschreiben eine Person oder eine Sache: **Gerald is careful.** Adverbien dagegen beschreiben, wie jemand etwas tut, oder wie etwas geschieht. Sie bestimmen z. B. Verben näher und werden meist aus Adjektiven gebildet.

Sehen Sie sich das Zitat an. Können Sie die folgende Regel zur Bildung von Adverbien ergänzen?

Adverbien bildet man, indem man die Endung **1.** ______ an ein Adjektiv anhängt. Endet ein Adjektiv auf **-y**, so wird das **-y** zu **-i: easy > easily**.

Aufgepasst: **hard** bleibt unverändert. Denn **hardly** heißt kaum:
He works hard. *Er arbeitet hart.*
Aber: **He hardly works.** *Er arbeitet kaum.*
Weitere Ausnahmen sind:
good > well
fast > fast
friendly > etwa: **in a friendly way**

Ergänzen Sie die Adverbien im Text mithilfe der Angaben in Klammern.

But Gerald was concentrating **2.** ______________ *(heavy)* on the small black box which he was taking **3.** ______________ *(quiet)* from his pocket. He stepped **4.** ______________ *(clumsy)*, then fell with a scream of surprise into the cold water of the river.

12. Verliebt – verlobt – verheiratet

Jetzt hat es Gerald geschafft. Er hat seiner Emma einen Antrag gemacht. Im Text kam bereits ein Ausdruck dafür vor. Erinnern Sie sich? Schreiben Sie ihn auf.

einen Antrag machen: ______________________________

Liebe kann so schön sein. Aber wie sagt man das auf Englisch? Wenn man sich verliebt, verfällt man der Liebe **to fall in love**, danach macht man einen Antrag **to propose to someone** und verlobt sich **to get engaged**. Ist man dann verlobt **to be engaged**, heiratet man auch irgendwann **to marry**. Hält die Ehe bis ans Lebensende, ist man **married for life**. Sollte die Ehe doch nicht halten, kann man sich scheiden lassen **to get divorced**.

Wie entwickelt sich also die Liebe? Bringen Sie die Schritte in die richtige Reihenfolge (manche Schritte können gleichzeitig stattfinden). Vom Anfang – bis zum Ende...

___ **A** to get engaged

___ **B** to fall in love

___ **C** to get divorced

___ **D** to be married for life

___ **E** to propose to someone

___ **F** to be engaged

___ **G** to get married

Richtige Reihenfolge: ______________________

7. It Could be Worse

Duncan **tried** not to look at his wife **while** he read his newspaper, but he knew that she was looking directly at him, and he knew that she was not happy.

tried - *versuchte*
while - *während*

"It could be worse," he said quietly, not looking at her cold, angry, blue eyes.

She was a small woman with short brown hair, a tiny nose and a kind smile. When she was happy, Duncan thought that she was possibly the most beautiful woman in the world, but when she was angry, Duncan thought that she was **terrifying**.

terrifying - *furchteinflößend*

"What?" Liz asked. "What did you say?"

They were sitting opposite each other at a small table in a tiny caravan. Inside the caravan there was one tiny bed, a tiny oven and a tiny window which was covered by an old white **curtain**. It was so small that even Liz could not stand up straight.

curtain - *Vorhang*

"I said, well, you know, it could be worse."

"How?" asked Liz. "How could this be worse? It's our ten year **wedding anniversary**. You promised me a **romantic**, **exotic** location, but instead we're in the middle of the Lake District in the smallest caravan in the world!"

wedding anniversary - *Hochzeitstag*
romantic - *romantisch*
exotic - *exotisch*

"This is romantic," Duncan **argued**. "You saw those fantastic hills, those beautiful lakes, those green forests. And the location is perfect, right next to Lake Windermere. **Go on** Liz, look at the view," he said, moving the curtain to reveal the countryside.

argued - *argumentierte*
go on - *na los, komm schon*

however - *jedoch*

The countryside, **however**, was not visible, because large black clouds were now covering the fantastic mountains, the beautiful lakes and the green forests.

"Oh," said Duncan, then he looked at his wife again. "But it could be worse, it's not…"

a loud crash of thunder - *ein lauter Donnerschlag*

determined - *entschlossen*

But before he could finish speaking there was **a loud crash of thunder**, and it began to rain.

His wife's face was terrifying, but Duncan was **determined** to be positive about the situation. "Well, a little rain is no problem for us. We're warm and dry in here, so we can watch the storm, open a bottle of wine. Quite romantic, really."

suddenly - *plötzlich*

holes - *Löcher*

Liz opened her mouth to speak, but **suddenly** stopped as a drip of water fell onto her head. Looking up they saw that the rain was falling through several small **holes** in the roof of the caravan.

"It's not a problem," Duncan said. "I can easily fix that. You open the wine. I'll be back in a minute." ▶▷▶

1. A trip to Lake Windermere

Haben Sie den Text aufmerksam gelesen? Beantworten Sie dann die folgenden Fragen. Mehrere Antworten können richtig sein.

1. Why doesn't Duncan look at his wife?

❍ **A** He's busy reading.

❍ **B** He knows that she is angry.

❍ **C** She is not inside the caravan.

2. What does Liz look like when she is angry?

❍ **A** Still beautiful.

❍ **B** She looks like a banshee.

❍ **C** She looks terrifying.

3. What do you know about the caravan?

❍ **A** It's luxurious.

❍ **B** It's brand new.

❍ **C** It's tiny.

4. How many years have the two been married?

❍ **A** 5 years.

❍ **B** 10 years.

❍ **C** 1 year.

5. Why is the countryside not visible?

❍ **A** It's night.

❍ **B** The curtains are closed.

❍ **C** The weather is too bad.

6. Why is the rain a problem?

❍ **A** They wanted to barbecue.

❍ **B** They wanted to go hiking.

❍ **C** There are holes in the roof of the caravan.

"This is romantic," Duncan argued. "You saw those fantastic hills, those beautiful lakes, those green forests. And the location is perfect, right next to Lake Windermere."

„Das ist romantisch", argumentierte Duncan. „Du hast doch diese fantastischen Hügel, diese wunderbaren Seen und diese grünen Wälder gesehen. Und unsere Lage ist perfekt, direkt am Lake Windermere."

2. Let's go camping

Was braucht man alles für einen gemütlichen Campingausflug? Ordnen Sie die Wörter den passenden Bildern zu:

1

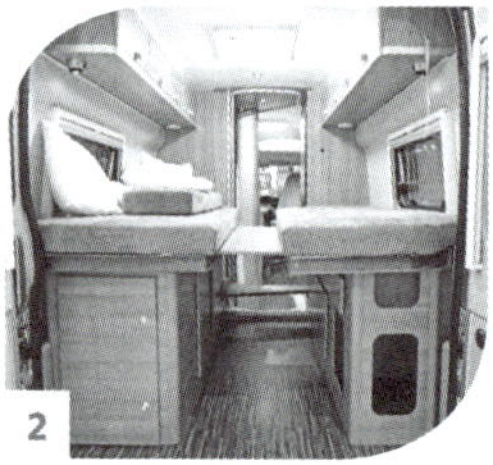
2

3

4

5

6

___ **A** camp bed

___ **B** camping cooker

___ **C** tent

___ **D** sleeping bag

___ **E** caravan

___ **F** countryside

3. In a thunderstorm

Liz und Duncan haben offensichtlich die Wettervorhersage nicht gehört. Kennen Sie die wichtigsten Wörter, die in einem Wetterbericht vorkommen können? Lesen Sie zuerst den Wetterbericht und schreiben Sie dann die hervorgehobenen Wörter zum passenden Bild.

Weather forecast for Lake Windermere:
Unfortunately, thick clouds are covering the sky. Within the next few minutes, a thunderstorm with very strong winds will develop. Frequent lightning must be expected. The area is caught by heavy rain, which can cause sudden dangerous floods.
If possible, stay inside.

1

____

2

____

3

____

4

____

5

____

4. Will-Future

Duncan verspricht Liz, dass er gleich zurück sein wird. Er verwendet für seine Aussage das *will-future*.

Können Sie mithilfe des Zitats die Regel für die Bildung des *will-future* vervollständigen?

"It's not a problem," Duncan said. "I can easily fix that. You open the wine. I'll be back in a minute."

„Das ist nicht schlimm", sagte Duncan. „Ich kann das ganz leicht reparieren. Mach du schon mal den Wein auf. Ich bin in einer Minute zurück."

Das **will-future** wird gebildet aus:

1. ____________ (not) + **2.** ____________.

I will fix the caravan. *Ich werde den Wohnwagen reparieren.*

She will not / won't stay here. *Sie wird nicht hier bleiben.*

They will get wet. *Sie werden nass werden.*

Das **will-future** wird bei Vorhersagen, Vermutungen und spontanen Entschlüssen verwendet. Deshalb sagt Duncan auch **"I will be back."**

Jetzt sind Sie dran! Setzen Sie folgende Sätze ins *will-future:*

3. She opened the wine.

____

4. A little rain is no problem for us.

____

5. Opposites

Das Campingwochenende ist das genaue Gegenteil von dem, was Liz sich erhofft hatte. Wie lauten die Eigenschaften, die auf den Bildern dargestellt sind? Ordnen Sie zu.

1

2

3

4

5

__ **A** warm __ **B** romantic __ **C** dry

__ **D** comfortable __ **E** happy

Wie lautet nun jeweils das Gegenteil dieser Adjektive? Der Buchstabensalat hilft Ihnen bei der Lösung.

6. warm ⟷ ______________________ (ldoc)

7. romantic ⟷ ______________________ (ictnaunmor)

8. dry ⟷ ______________________ (tew)

9. huge ⟷ ______________________ (ynti)

10. happy ⟷ ______________________ (ppyunha)

Ob es Duncan wohl gelingt, das Dach zu reparieren und den Ausflug zu retten?

expression – *Ausdruck*

was pouring down – *fiel in Strömen*

dripping wet – *patschnass*

he was determined – *er war entschlossen*

a strange noise – *ein seltsames Geräusch*

squeaking – *quietschend*

Liz was silent, but the **expression** on her face made Duncan quickly move to the tiny door and push it open. The rain **was pouring down** now, the dark clouds covering the hills on each side of the impressive Lake Windermere.

It was beautiful, Duncan thought, and if he could repair the roof quickly, he was sure that Liz would enjoy the holiday.

Moving to the side of the small caravan he lifted his leg and began to climb up onto the roof. In only a few seconds he was **dripping wet**, but **he was determined** to make his poor wife happy.

Carefully, he moved across to where the holes were and saw the problem. "It's not too bad," he shouted, "I think I can fix it if I move this. Yes, it could be worse!" And he began to move a piece of plastic into position.

It was then, however, that he heard **a strange noise** from under his feet. For just a second more he stood there. Then, with a terrible crash, he fell through the roof and landed in the middle of the caravan.

Liz screamed and dropped the bottle of wine that she was holding. "Duncan, are you okay?" she asked as she looked at him on the floor.

"I think so," he said, checking that his arms and legs could still move. "Yes, I'm okay, nothing broken…so it could be…"

But before Duncan could finish his sentence there was another noise, a quiet, **squeaking** noise.

"What's that?" asked Liz.

"Probably nothing, but maybe we should..."

Suddenly, the caravan began to move.

"Get out!" shouted Liz, then she ran to the tiny door, pushed it open and jumped out.

Duncan was a little slower, because the caravan was now moving much faster, and twice he fell while he tried to move to the door.

"Duncan! Jump!" he heard Liz shout, but before he could push the door open there was a loud **splash** as the caravan rolled into the water of the impressive Lake Windermere.

For a moment he did nothing as the cold water of the lake filled the tiny caravan, but as it began to cover his legs he **recovered from his shock**, reached up to the hole in the roof and **pulled himself up**.

"Are you okay?" Liz shouted from the side of the lake.

Duncan thought about his reply, only for a moment. Then he smiled as he rested on the roof of the **sinking** caravan. "It could be worse."

And for the first time that day he saw his wife smile, and he thought that she was **possibly** the most beautiful woman in the world. ■

splash – *Platschen*

recovered from his shock – *er erholte sich von seinem Schock*

pulled himself up – *zog sich hoch*

sinking – *sinkend*

possibly – *vermutlich*

6. What is correct?

Kreuzen Sie die Aussagen an, die mit der Geschichte übereinstimmen.

1. ❍ **A** The weather was getting better.
❍ **B** The weather was bad: it was raining heavily.

2. ❍ **A** Duncan climbs onto the caravan without a ladder.
❍ **B** Duncan borrows a ladder to climb onto the caravan.

3. ❍ **A** Duncan can fix the roof.
❍ **B** Duncan falls through the broken roof.

4. ❍ **A** Duncan is ok. He didn't break a leg or an arm.
❍ **B** Duncan breaks his leg.

5. ❍ **A** Suddenly, they get help from other people.
❍ **B** Suddenly, the caravan starts to move.

6. ❍ **A** The caravan rolls into the lake, but Duncan and Liz are happy.
❍ **B** The caravan is fixed and Duncan and Liz are happy.

Gut, dass die Geschichte noch humorvoll endet. **Lake Windermere** liegt im **Lake District** und ist in der Tat eine der beliebtesten englischen Ferienregionen aufgrund seiner wunderschönen Landschaft. Der See ist übrigens der größte Natursee Englands. Wenn man darin ein Bad nimmt, ist es schon etwas Besonderes, und wenn man auch noch so eine abenteuerliche Geschichte dazu erzählen kann, wie Liz und Duncan, dann ist der 10. Hochzeitstag auf jeden Fall unvergesslich.

7. Unregelmäßige Adjektive steigern

Die regelmäßige Steigerung der Adjektive durch Anhängen von **-er / -est** und mit **more / most** haben Sie bereits in Lektion 3 gelernt.

Einige regelmäßige Adjektive haben Besonderheiten in der Schreibweise:

happy *(glücklich)* **- happier - (the) happiest**
big *(groß)* **- bigger - (the) biggest**
nice *(nett)* **- nicer - (the) nicest**

Einige Adjektive haben allerdings eine unregelmäßige Steigerung:

good *(gut)* **- better - (the) best**
bad *(schlecht)* **- worse - (the) worst**
much *(viel)* **- more - (the) most** (bei unzählbaren Substantiven)
many *(viele)* **- more - (the) most -** (bei zählbaren Substantiven)
little *(wenig, bei Mengen)* **- less - (the) least**
little *(klein, bei Größen)* **- smaller - (the) smallest**

"It's not too bad (...) Yes, it could be worse!"

„Es ist nicht so schlimm (...) Ja, es könnte schlimmer sein!"

Um bei zählbaren Mengen *wenig* anzugeben, verwenden Sie nicht **little**, sondern **few**, was regelmäßig gesteigert wird: **few, fewer, (the) fewest**.

Und so bilden Sie die Steigerung:

- Bei Gleichheit: **as** + Grundform des Adjektivs + **as**
  The caravan is as old as Duncan. *(...so alt wie...)*
- Bei Ungleichheit: Komparativ + **than**
  Duncan is happier than Liz. *(...glücklicher als...)*

Vervollständigen Sie folgenden Text mit den passenden Formen der in Klammern angegebenen Adjektive:

Unfortunately, the weather was **1.** ______________ *(bad)* than expected.

What Duncan hadn't expected was the **2.** ______________ *(bad)* case: that the caravan would break down completely. But after the accident, his and Liz's mood was a lot **3.** ______________ *(good)* than before.

8. Adverbien steigern

Auch Adverbien werden durch **-er / -est** bzw. mit **more / most** gesteigert.
Und bei den Adverbien gibt es auch unregelmäßige Steigerungsformen, z. B.:
(Adjektiv: **good** *gut*) Adverb: **well - better - best**
(Adjektiv: **bad** *schlecht*) Adverb: **badly - worse - worst**
(Adjektiv: **much** *viel*) Adverb: **much - more - most**
(Adjektiv: **little** *wenig*) Adverb: **little - less - least**

Vervollständigen Sie nun den Text mit den passenden Adverbien in der passenden Form.

Liz scolded *(schimpfte)* Duncan **1.** ______________ *(bad)* for taking her to such a terrible place. Everything seemed to go wrong, and she was even **2.** ______________ *(little)* amused when it suddenly started to rain inside the caravan.

Looking back, however, she liked it **3.** ______________ *(good)* when they were outside in the rain with the caravan in the lake. This final disaster was so funny that it made her laugh after all.

9. Adjektiv oder Adverb?

**Duncan möchte das Dach reparieren und tut sein Bestes.
Überlegen Sie, ob im folgenden Text die Substantive näher beschrieben werden oder die Handlungen, d. h. ob Sie ein Adjektiv oder ein Adverb einsetzen müssen!**

Duncan hoped that he could **1.** ______________________ *(quick)* repair the roof of the caravan. He **2.** ______________________ *(careful)* climbed onto the roof. He had always been a very **3.** ______________________ *(athletic)* man, so it was not a real problem for him. Unfortunately, the roof was **4.** ______________________ *(terrible)* wet, so it was **5.** ______________________ *(hard)* for Duncan not to fall. In the end, however, he fell, but it was not his fault. The roof was **6.** ______________________ *(heavy)* damaged, so it broke and Duncan fell into the caravan. The caravan started to roll and rolled **7.** ______________________ *(slow)* right into the lake. Thank God, both Liz and Duncan were very **8.** ______________________ *(clever)* and jumped off the caravan right in time. Funnily enough, Liz was now **9.** ______________________ *(little)* angry than before.

Ein Adverb kann ein Verb, ein Adjektiv, ein anderes Adverb oder einen ganzen Satz näher beschreiben.
Hier bezieht sich ein Adverb auf ein anderes Adverb:
They laughed extremely hard. *Sie mussten furchtbar heftig lachen.*
In der Übung oben finden Sie Beispiele für die anderen Anwendungen eines Adverbs. Vergleichen Sie die Sätze mit den Lösungen.

10. Das Partizip Präsens

Das Partizip Präsens (**present participle** oder ing-Form) drückt eine aktive Handlung aus. Es wird im Englischen mit **Verb + -ing** gebildet und ist personenunabhängig. Im Deutschen findet sich oft die Endung *-end* am Verb:

laughing > *lachend*, **coming >** *kommend*, **dripping >** *tropfend*

Die betreffende Handlung kann aber auch - im Englischen wie im Deutschen - durch einen Nebensatz a

... while he was checking that ...
(...während er überprüfte, ob...).

"I think so," he said, checking that his arms and legs could still move.

„Ich glaube schon," sagte er, während er überprüfte, ob er seine Arme und Beine noch bewegen konnte.

Lesen Sie den Text noch einmal durch. Können Sie die darin vorkommenden Partizipien mit folgenden deutschen Bedeutungen finden? Tipp: Das *present participle* tritt auch in *Continuous*-Formen auf, sowie als Adjektiv.

1. c____________________ *(bedeckend)*

2. sq____________________ *(quietschend)*

3. s____________________ *(sinkend)*

4. m____________________ *(sich bewegend)*

Wandeln Sie jetzt die hervorgehobenen Satzteile in ein Partizip um:

5. **He lifted his leg and** began to climb onto the roof.

____

6. **Liz screamed and** dropped the bottle of wine she was holding.

____

11. If-Satz Typ I + II (Bedingungssätze)

In der Geschichte finden sich zwei Sätze wieder, in denen das Wort *if* vorkommt. Finden Sie die Sätze und schreiben Sie sie auf:

1. ______________________________
2. ______________________________

If bedeutet *wenn, falls*. **If**-Sätze leiten einen Nebensatz ein und enthalten eine Bedingung für den Hauptsatz. Verwendet man sie, muss man darauf achten, ob die Bedingung vermutlich erfüllt werden kann (Typ I) oder nicht (Typ II). Denn dies wird durch verschiedene Zeitformen ausgedrückt.
Wichtig: Die Zeitformen dürfen innerhalb der Sätze **nicht** vertauscht werden!
Sehen Sie sich die Regeln und die Beispielsätze an:

Typ I: erfüllbare Bedingung

if*-Satz im *present tense	**Hauptsatz: *will / can* + Infinitiv**
If the weather is fine,	**we can / will have a picnic.**
Wenn das Wetter gut ist,	*können / werden wir ein Picknick machen.*

Typ II: nicht / kaum erfüllbare Bedingung

if*-Satz im *simple past	**Hauptsatz: *could / would* + Infinitiv**
If it stopped raining,	**we could go for a walk.**
Wenn es aufhörte / aufhören würde zu regnen,	*könnten wir spazierengehen.*

Übrigens, mit **would** oder **could** können auch höfliche Bitten, Fragen oder Vorschläge ausgedrückt werden.
Could you help me, please? *Könntest du / Könnten Sie mir bitte helfen?*
Would you like a glass of wine? *Hättest du / Hätten Sie gern ein Glas Wein?*

12. Would you...?

Ordnen Sie zuerst die Bilder den Sätzen zu.

1

2

3

4

Welche Sprechabsicht drücken die Sätze aus? Ordnen Sie die Sprechabsichten den Sätzen zu.

höfliche Bitten • Bedingungssätze (*if*-Sätze) • höfliche Fragen • höfliche Vorschläge

___ **A** Which kind of anniversary holiday would you choose?

____

___ **B** If the roof of the caravan wasn't so damaged, Duncan would be able to fix it.

____

___ **C** Could you help me up, please?

____

___ **D** Would you like to go to a hotel?

____

13. Typ I oder Typ II?

Für welchen Typ *if*-Satz, d. h. für welche Zeitformen je Satzteil müssen Sie sich hier jeweils entscheiden?

Liz hopes: "If the roof **1.** ______________________ *(collapse)*, we **2.** ______________________ *(can go)* to a hotel. But I suppose this will not happen because Duncan is good at fixing things."
Duncan thinks: "If I **3.** ______________________ *(cannot fix)* the roof, I **4.** ______________________ *(take)* Liz to a hotel. I'm sure we will be in a hotel very soon because the roof looks awful."

14. When or if?

***When* und *if* bedeuten beide *wenn*. Trotzdem werden sie unterschiedlich angewendet. Worin besteht der Unterschied bei den folgenden Sätzen?**

If we ever go camping again, we won't take a caravan.
Der Sprecher ist sich **1.** ______________________ *(sicher / nicht sicher)*, ob er jemals wieder zum Campen gehen möchte.
When we go camping next May, we take a tent.
Der Sprecher ist sich **2.** ______________________ (sicher / nicht sicher), dass er wieder zum Campen gehen möchte.

***If* oder *when*? Entscheiden Sie, welches der beiden Wörtchen bei den folgenden Sätzen passt.**

Duncan thinks: **3.** ______________________ I don't fix that roof soon, Liz will get really angry.
Liz thinks: **4.** ______________________ Duncan gets back inside, I tell him that I love him, **5.** ______________________ he doesn't fall off the roof before.

15. What a mess!

Was für ein Durcheinander! Verbinden Sie die Satzanfänge und Satzenden wieder richtig miteinander:

1. If Liz asked Duncan,

2. If the caravan can be repaired,

3. When Liz is happy,

4. If they were rich,

5. When they get home,

6. When Liz was angry

- **A** she is possibly the most beautiful woman in the world.
- **B** they could buy a new caravan.
- **C** she was terrifying.
- **D** will Liz go camping with Duncan again?
- **E** would he take her to a hotel?
- **F** they will have a story to tell.

16. It could be worse ...

Was könnte Liz in den folgenden Situationen antworten? Ordnen Sie die Redewendungen zu. Manchmal sind auch mehrere möglich.

never mind • it doesn't matter • don't worry • no problem • it could be worse

1. Duncan spills *(verschüttet)* some wine across Liz's trousers. She isn't angry about it and says: ______________________

2. Duncan is afraid that the weekend could harm their relationship. Liz wants to calm him and says: ______________________

3. Duncan asks Liz whether she can get the wine out of her trousers. She says:

____

4. Both are in a good mood. No weather can harm them. Liz thinks:

____

5. Now, Liz pours Duncan a glass of wine. He thanks her. She answers:

____

8. Don't Panic!

"*Don't panic*! That's the important thing! Just don't panic!"

The old Mini is in the middle of a narrow country road. Its engine is on, but for the moment it is not moving. It is a small *red dot of colour* in the middle of the white snow storm.

"I'm not panicking, *Darling*," says Bethan, the young woman sitting in the passenger seat of the car. "But, darling do you know where we are?"

"Do I know where we are? Do I know where we are?" says Matthew, her husband. "This is where I'm from, Bethan. This is my family home. I know these hills and forests *like the back of my hand*."

Bethan, who is a very *calm* young lady with short brown hair, gentle eyes and a kind smile, *nods her head*. "Great, so where are we?"

Matthew, who is a tall and thin young man who becomes nervous quickly looks out of the window. "Well, I don't know! I can't see a thing!"

Bethan nods her head calmly. "Okay, but we want to go to your old village. What's it called?"

"New Inn, it's called New Inn. But I can't see any *road signs* to tell us where it is. My mother is not going to be happy. She hates

don't panic! – *Nur keine Panik!*

red dot of colour – *roter Farbklecks*

darling – *Liebling*

like the back of my hand – *wie meine Westentasche*

calmly – *ruhig*

nods her head – *nickt mit dem Kopf*

road signs – *Straßenschilder*

it when people are late. She normally *serves* Christmas lunch at two. What time is it?"

"We don't know, Darling. Remember, the clock is *broken*," Bethan replies.

"Oh yes, well let's turn on the radio for a moment. Here we go…"

For a second *nothing happens*, but then they hear a familiar female voice. "The Queen's speech," says Bethan. "Oh no, it must be three o'clock."

"Don't panic! I'm going to phone them and ask them to…"

"No Darling, remember, we can't get a signal."

Matthew hits his head against the *steering wheel in despair*. "Oh! I forgot!" he shouts, then hits his head against the steering wheel three more times.

"Fine, okay," he says after a minute. "I'm going to drive until we see a sign, or a house, or something."

"Good idea," says Bethan. "And Darling, do you think you can drive quickly?"

Matthew *shakes his head*. "Not in this snow. Why?"

Bethan looks down at her large, pregnant *stomach*, then turns to her husband. "Because I think my *waters have broken*." ▶▷▶

serves - *serviert*
broken - *kaputt*
nothing happens - *nichts passiert*
steering wheel - *Lenkrad*
in despair - *verzweifelt*
shakes his head - *schüttelt seinen Kopf*
stomach - *Bauch*
my waters have broken - *meine Fruchtblase ist geplatzt*

1. A trip in a snow storm

Haben Sie den Text aufmerksam gelesen? Beantworten Sie dann die folgenden Fragen. Mehrere Antworten können richtig sein.

1. Where do Bethan and Matthew want to go?

❍ **A** To hospital.

❍ **B** To Matthew's mother.

❍ **C** To a friend.

2. Why did they get lost?

❍ **A** Because of the snow storm.

❍ **B** Because they don't use a map.

❍ **C** Because the navigation system broke down.

3. Why is Matthew's mother not going to be happy?

❍ **A** She doesn't like Bethan.

❍ **B** They are going to be late.

❍ **C** They forgot to bring presents.

4. What time is it?

❍ **A** Three o'clock.

❍ **B** Four o'clock.

❍ **C** Five o'clock.

5. Why can't they use the phone?

❍ **A** The phone was stolen.

❍ **B** They forgot the phone at home.

❍ **C** They can't get a signal.

6. Why does Bethan want Matthew to go faster?

❍ **A** She's having her baby.

❍ **B** She's hungry.

❍ **C** She needs to go to the toilet.

Heutzutage hat fast jeder im Auto auch sein Handy dabei. Das deutsche Wort *Handy* klingt zwar englisch, ist es aber nicht: Im Englischen lautet die richtige Bezeichnung **mobile (phone)** oder auch **(smart) phone**, im amerikanischen Englisch heißt es auch **cell (phone)**.
Kann man sein Handy mit einer Freisprecheinrichtung benutzen, sagt man: **I'm using a hands-free phone**.

2. *In the car*

Die werdenden Eltern sind mit dem Auto unterwegs. Ordnen Sie die Autoteile auf den Bildern den passenden Wörtern zu.

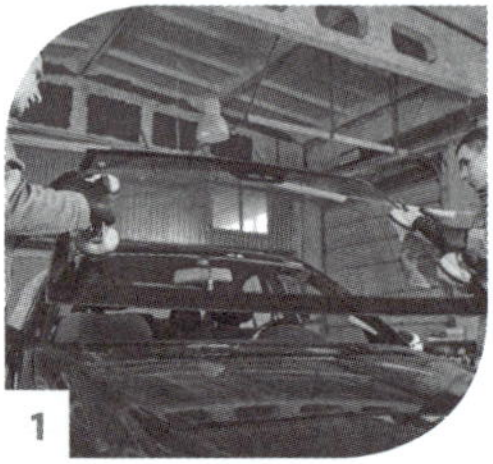
1

2

3

4

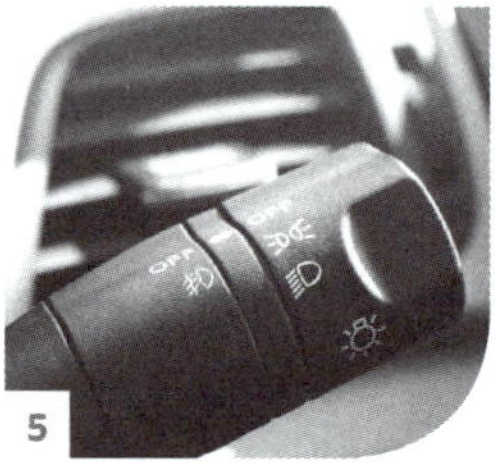
5

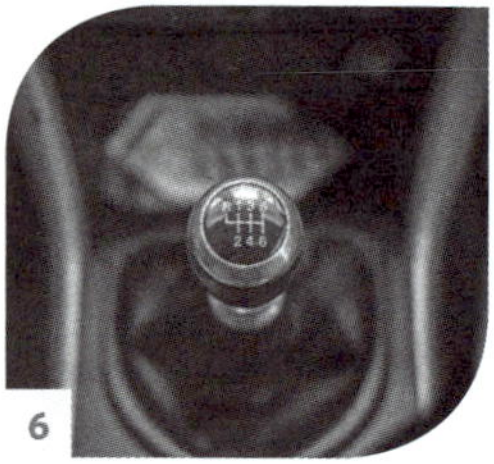
6

___ **A** steering wheel

___ **B** windscreen

___ **C** gear stick

___ **E** handbrake

___ **D** indicator

___ **F** seatbelt

3. Es ist Winter

Die beiden sind mitten im Winter unterwegs – und das ausgerechnet bei einem Schneesturm. Womit muss man im Winter rechnen, wenn man mit dem Auto unterwegs ist? Ordnen Sie die Wörter den Bildern zu.

1

2

3

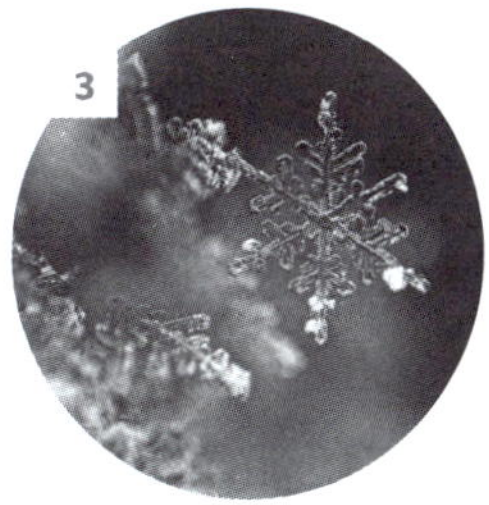

4

5

___ **B** black ice

___ **A** snowflake

___ **C** avalanche

___ **D** icicle

___ **E** snowplough

4. *On the phone*

Bethan versucht zu telefonieren, doch leider hat sie keinen Empfang. Was braucht man zum Telefonieren? Ordnen Sie zu.

1. mobile phone	**A** Anbieter
2. signal	**B** Bildschirm
3. keypad	**C** Empfang
4. display	**D** Tastatur
5. provider	**E** Handy

5. *Was gehört alles zu Weihnachten?*

Leider sind die Buchstaben durcheinander geraten. Entwirren Sie sie und finden Sie heraus, was alles zu Weihnachten dazugehört.

1. wnos ______________________ *(Schnee)*

2. repsnets ______________________ *(Geschenke)*

3. teomislte ______________________ *(Mistelzweig)*

4. mastsichr dsarc ______________________ *(Weihnachtskarten)*

5. mastsichr eret ______________________ *(Weihnachtsbaum)*

In Großbritannien werden die Geschenke nicht am Heiligabend, dem **Christmas Eve**, sondern erst am 25. Dezember, dem **Christmas Day**, in der Früh geöffnet. Traditionell gibt es Truthahn oder Gans mit Kartoffeln und Rosenkohl. Als Glücksbringer hängt man einen Mistelzweig auf. Der 26. Dezember heißt **Boxing Day**, da früher die Angestellten an diesem Tag eine Geschenkbox von ihrem Arbeitgeber erhielten. Heute ist es ein verkaufsoffener Feiertag mit Sonderpreisen.

6. Mixed bag

Was denkt sich Matthew, als Bethan ihm erzählt, dass ihre Fruchtblase geplatzt ist? Ergänzen Sie die Geschichte und achten Sie dabei darauf, die richtigen Zeiten in den Lücken zu verwenden. Folgende Zeiten kommen vor.

will-Future • **going to-Future** • **simple present** (2x) • **simple past** (2x)

Oh my God! I **1.** ____________________ *(be)* a father soon.
I **2.** ____________________ *(be)* so nervous! Bethan
3. ____________________ *(be)* such a wonderful person.
I **4.** ____________________ *(fall)* in love with her immediately
when I **5.** ____________________ *(meet)* her three years ago.
I just hope that our kid **6.** ____________________ *(be)* more like
her than like me.

Bethan hat recht: Um 15 Uhr bzw. 3 p.m. wird jedes Jahr am 25. Dezember die **Queen's Christmas Message** – die Weihnachtsansprache der Königin – im Fernsehen übertragen. Für diese Rede wählt die Königin selbst das Thema aus, im Gegensatz zur **Queen's Speech**, die sie feierlich vom Thron im Oberhaus verliest und womit sie das neue Parlamentsjahr eröffnet. Der Inhalt der **Queen's Speech** wird von der Regierung zusammengestellt und enthält eine Zusammenfassung ihrer politischen Vorhaben für die neue Sitzungsperiode. Nichtsdestotrotz ist die **Queen's Christmas Message** informell als die **Queen's Speech** bekannt.

Jetzt wird es brenzlig. Ob die beiden es wohl rechtzeitig schaffen? Oder kommt das Baby im Auto zur Welt?

becomes – *(hier:) nimmt ... an*
quietly – *ruhig*
midwife – *Hebamme*
is about to – *will gerade*
strange light – *seltsames Licht*
It must be another car – *Es muss ein anderes Auto sein*
Careful! – *Vorsichtig!*
someone's out there – *jemand ist dort draußen*
is having a baby – *bekommt gerade ein Kind*
we are completely lost – *wir wissen überhaupt nicht, wo wir sind*

▶▷▶ Matthew's face *becomes* the colour of the snow storm. "Your…waters…have…"

"Now Darling, remember; don't panic," Bethan *quietly* says.

"Your waters have broken! Oh my God! We need to go to the hospital, or to my mother's house! She's a *midwife*! She knows what to do!"

"I know, Darling, but where *is* your mother's house?"

Matthew *is about to* hit his head against the steering wheel again when suddenly, in the middle of the snow storm, they see a *strange light*.

"A light!" Matthew shouts. "What is it? A star? No, *it must be another car*. Okay, I'm going to follow it!"

And he quickly drives the car forwards.

"*Careful!*" a voice shouts.

"Stop!" Bethan says. "I think *someone's out there*!"

Matthew stops the car and opens his window. Outside, covered in snow, are three mountain bikers; each with a bright light on the front of their bike.

"You nearly hit us!" the first mountain biker shouts.

"I'm very sorry!" says Matthew. "But my wife *is having a baby* and *we are completely lost*!"

The second mountain biker looks into the window of the Mini and smiles at Bethan. "On Christmas day? In a snow storm? Well, don't panic, just tell us where you want to go."

"To my mother's house!" Matthew shouts. "She's a midwife. She lives at New Inn. Do you know the village? Can you help us?"

For a moment there is silence, then the third mountain biker moves *forward* and looks at Matthew's face. "Matthew Griffiths? Is that you? *You daft fool*! Look where you are! This is New Inn! Your mother's house is twenty metres *down the road*!" The three mountain bikers begin to laugh, but Matthew says nothing to them. *Instead*, very calmly he turns to Bethan and smiles. "See, *I told you* not to panic."

forward – *vorwärts*
you daft fool! – *du blöder Idiot!*
down the road – *die Straße hinunter*
instead – *stattdessen*
I told you – *Ich habe es dir gesagt*

7. Right or wrong?

Haben Sie den zweiten Teil grob verstanden? Dann testen Sie es mal. Kreuzen Sie an, ob folgende Aussagen richtig oder falsch sind.

		RIGHT	WRONG
1.	Matthew's mother is a midwife.	❍	❍
2.	The light they see belongs to another car.	❍	❍
3.	The people they meet know New Inn.	❍	❍
4.	They only have 10 more minutes to drive.	❍	❍
5.	Bethan has her baby in the car.	❍	❍

Sicher hat Bethan schon eine **Baby Shower** hinter sich, eine Feier für die werdende Mutter. Dieser Brauch kommt aus den USA, wird aber auch in Großbritannien und immer öfter auch in Deutschland gefeiert. Er entstand im 19. Jahrhundert, als Freundinnen für die werdende Mutter am Nachmittag eine **Tea Party** gaben, bei der man unter eleganten Schirmen im Garten saß. Geschenke wurden übrigens erst nach dem 2. Weltkrieg in den USA üblich.

8. Ordnungszahlen

Die zwei treffen auf drei Mountainbiker. Lesen Sie im Text nach und ergänzen Sie die Ordnungszahlen.

1. The ____________________ mountain biker shouts.

2. The ____________________ mountain biker looks into the window.

3. The ____________________ mountain biker moves forward.

Die ersten drei Ordnungszahlen und die Ordnungszahl zur 5 **(five > fifth)** und zur 12 **(twelve > twelfth)** werden unregelmäßig gebildet.

Können Sie den Satz zur regelmäßigen Bildung von Ordnungszahlen ergänzen?

Ordnungszahlen werden gebildet, indem man **4.** - ____________________ an die reguläre Zahl anhängt.

Ergänzen Sie folgenden Text jeweils mit den korrekt geschriebenen Ordnungszahlen (s. Angaben nach den Lücken).

Matthew, this is the **5.** ____________________ (3.) time I've told you not to panic. Darling, this is the **6.** ____________________ (1.) time we are having a baby, and I don't want to have our baby in the car. But it won't help if you hit the steering wheel for the **7.** ____________________ (8.) time.

Übrigens: Bei Zahlen, die auf **-y** enden, wird das **-y** durch **-ieth** ersetzt:
twenty > **twentieth, thirty** > **thirtieth** etc.
Und: Bei Zahlwörtern, die auf **-t** enden, entfällt dieses:
eight > **eighth**

9. To have a baby

Welche Begriffe, die mit Schwangerschaft zu tun haben, können Sie in der Geschichte finden? Suchen Sie die Begriffe aus der gesamten Geschichte heraus und schreiben Sie sie zur Übersetzung.

1. ______________________________ *(großer, schwangerer Bauch)*

2. ______________________________ *(meine Fruchtblase ist geplatzt)*

3. ______________________________ *(Krankenhaus)*

4. ______________________________ *(Hebamme)*

5. ______________________________ *(ein Baby bekommen)*

10. The baby has arrived

Wenn das Baby erst einmal da ist, braucht man bestimmte Dinge. Ordnen Sie die Bilder den Begriffen zu.

1

2

3

4

5

6

___ **A** dummy ___ **B** baby bottle ___ **C** pram

___ **D** nappies ___ **E** cot ___ **F** Babygro®

11. Müssen und sollen

We need to go to the hospital...!

Wir müssen ins Krankenhaus...!

Nachdem ihre Fruchtblase geplatzt ist, sollten Matthew und Bethan ins Krankenhaus fahren ...

Um Notwendigkeit auszudrücken, gibt es im Englischen drei Möglichkeiten:

must: Der Sprecher / die Sprecherin selbst hält etwas für notwendig. Es wird ein starker Zwang oder eine Verpflichtung ausgedrückt.

I must stay calm.
Ich muss ruhig bleiben.

have to: Hiermit wird ein Zwang von außen ausgedrückt, z. B. durch eine Anordnung oder ein Gesetz.

You have to pay taxes for your car.
Sie müssen Steuern für Ihr Auto bezahlen.

need to: Dies ist die schwächste Form, um auszudrücken, dass etwas nötig ist bzw. getan werden sollte.

We need to shovel. The entrance is already covered with snow again.
Wir sollten schippen! Die Einfahrt ist schon wieder mit Schnee bedeckt.

Setzen Sie jetzt die passenden Wörter in die Lücken ein.

Matthew says to Bethan: "You absolutely **1.** ____________ remain calm. Everything is going to be ok. I realize that I **2.** ____________ ask for the way because we **3.** ____________ take you to my mum soon. But don't panic, I know what to do."

12. Can vs. may

Can you help us?

Können Sie uns helfen?

Matthew, der verständlicherweise ziemlich nervös ist, bittet um Hilfe.

Worin besteht der Unterschied in den folgenden Sätzen?

Can the mountain bikers help Matthew? *Können die Mountainbiker...*

They can, but they may be late for their own Christmas dinner then.

Sie können, aber sie verspäten sich dann möglicherweise...

Can und **may** sind (wie **must** und **need**) Modalverben, d. h. Hilfsverben, die die Bedeutung des Hauptverbs modifizieren (= abwandeln). Sie haben eine ähnliche Bedeutung. Mit **can** drückt man jedoch eine Fähigkeit aus, während **may** verwendet wird, wenn man über eine Möglichkeit spricht.

Füllen Sie in den folgenden Sätzen die Lücken mit dem korrekten Modalverb (*can* oder *may*) aus.

1. ______________________ you please ask the mountain bikers where we are?

2. They ______________________ not know it.

3. I don't think that I ______________________ go any further with my car.

4. I ______________________ not wait any longer. My waters have broken.
I have to see the midwife immediately.

5. I ______________________ even have to go to the hospital.

Matthew könnte auch zu Bethan sagen:
You mustn't panic. *Du darfst nicht in Panik geraten.*
Anders, als man es erwarten würde, bedeutet **must not** bzw. **mustn't** *nicht dürfen*. Will man ausdrücken, dass etwas nicht getan werden muss, verwendet man **need not** bzw. **needn't**:
Do I have to go to the hospital? – No, you don't have to. / No, you needn't. *Nein, du musst nicht / brauchst nicht.*

"I'm very sorry!" says Matthew.

„Es tut mir sehr leid!" sagt Matthew.

13. Reported speech

In dieser Geschichte wird sehr häufig direkte Rede wiedergegeben. Dadurch wirkt die Geschichte sehr lebendig und die Spannung erhöht sich. Diese direkte Rede lässt sich aber auch anders wiedergeben, nämlich mit **reported speech** *(indirekter Rede)*:

Matthew says (that) he is very sorry.

Der Text, der in Anführungszeichen stand, wird zu einem Folgesatz, der mit **that** eingeleitet werden kann (aber nicht muss). Davor steht ein Einleitungssatz mit einem Verb des Mitteilens (**say**, **tell** etc.) Bei der Übertragung in die indirekte Rede können sich die Personalpronomen verändern. In unserem Beispiel wurde aus

"I'm very sorry!" > ... he is very sorry.

Versuchen Sie es jetzt einmal. Übertragen Sie in die indirekte Rede, was Matthew über seine Mutter erzählt:

1. "My mother is not going to be happy."

____

2. "She hates it when people are late."

____

3. "She normally serves Christmas lunch at two."

____

Bezieht sich eine Aussage auf die Vergangenheit, steht das einleitende Verb im **simple past**. Die Zeit im Folgesatz versetzt man meist um eine Zeitstufe zurück: **He says to the bikers, "I'm glad to see you." > He said to the bikers that he was glad to see them.**

14. Imperative

"Don't panic!"
Keine Panik!

Unsere Geschichte beginnt mit einem Imperativ, einer Befehlsform. Mit dieser Verbform kann man Befehle, Aufforderungen, Verbote, Ratschläge, Wünsche oder Bitten ausdrücken. Man spricht damit eine oder mehrere Personen direkt an.

Sehen Sie sich diese Zitate an. Können Sie mit ihrer Hilfe die Regel zur Bildung des Imperativs ergänzen?

"Stop!" *"... just tell us where you want to go."* *"Look where you are!"*

Der Imperativ entspricht im Englischen der **1.** ______________________ des Verbs. Will man ein Verbot ausdrücken, setzt man **2.** ______________________ davor.

Bringen Sie jetzt die Satzteile in die richtige Reihenfolge.

3. in | please | come | , | .

____

4. Mum | forgot | tell | I | the way home | don't | .

____

Aufforderungen enden im Englischen mit einem Punkt. Nur bei besonders betonten Befehlen steht ein Ausrufezeichen.
Will man sich etwas höflicher ausdrücken, hängt man **please** an oder verwendet zusätzlich **could / would**:
Close the door, please. / Could you please close the door?

15. Das Present Perfect

Was sagt Bethan, als Ihre Fruchtblase geplatzt ist? Sehen Sie im Text nach und ergänzen Sie das Zitat.

My waters ______________________________.

Das Zitat steht im **present perfect**. Diese Zeitform drückt hier aus, dass das (vergangene) Geschehen für die Gegenwart wichtig ist bzw. sich darauf auswirkt. Das **present perfect** wird auch verwendet für

- Handlungen, die in der Vergangenheit begonnen haben und bis in die Gegenwart andauern (mit **since**, **for** *seit*)
- Handlungen, die gerade erst abgeschlossen wurden (mit **just** – *gerade eben*)
- Dinge, die noch nicht geschehen sind (mit **never** *nie*, **not ... yet** *noch nicht*)
- Fragen, ob etwas bisher schon bzw. schon einmal geschehen ist (mit **yet** *schon*, **ever** *jemals*)

Sehen Sie sich das Zitat noch einmal an. Können Sie die folgende Regel ergänzen?

Gebildet wird das **present perfect** mit:

1. __________ / **2.** __________ **(not) + Infinitiv** + **3.** -__________ (regelmäßige Verbform) oder **4.** ______________________________ Verbform.

Setzen Sie im folgenden Abschnitt die Verben in Klammern ins *present perfect*:

Matthew **5.** ______________________________ *(not / say)* anything yet, but the three mountain bikers **6.** ______________________________ *(begin)* to laugh. They **7.** ______________________________ *(just / remember)* him. They **8.** ______________________________ *(know)* him since their childhood.

16. Present Perfect oder Simple Past?

Nun ist das Baby auf der Welt. Entscheiden Sie, ob im folgenden Text jeweils das *present perfect* oder das *simple past* die richtige Zeit ist, und setzen Sie die Verben entsprechend ein.

When Bethan and Matthew **1.** ______________________ *(meet)* back in 2014, they **2.** ______________________ *(do not know)* that they would have a baby three years later.

"Matthew, **3.** ______________________ *(you / ever / see)* such a sweet baby as ours?"

"Bethan, I **4.** ______________________ *(just / think)* exactly the same. You know, three years ago, I **5.** ______________________ *(not / believe)* that I would ever have children. But then we **6.** ______________________ *(become)* a couple and since then, things **7.** ______________________ *(change)*."

Das deutsche Wort *seit* kann man mit **since** oder mit **for** übersetzen. **Since** verwendet man im **present perfect**, wenn man von einem Zeitpunkt spricht: **I've known him <u>since</u> 2014.** *Ich kenne* ihn seit 2014. **For** verwendet man im **present perfect**, wenn man von einem Zeitraum spricht: **I've known him <u>for</u> 3 years.** *Ich kenne ihn seit 3 Jahren.*

17. *When the kids get older*

Ehe man sich's versieht, sind aus Neugeborenen Erwachsene geworden. Ordnen Sie die passenden Begriffe den Fotos zu:

1

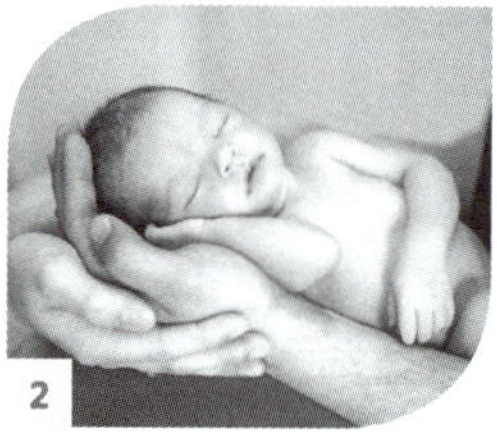
2

3

4

5

6

__ **A** newborn

__ **B** baby / infant

__ **C** toddler

__ **D** adult

__ **E** teenager

__ **F** child

Im Englischen gibt es verschiedene Begriffe, um über Babys und Kleinkinder zu sprechen. Ein Neugeborenes ist ein **newborn** oder man spricht vom **baby** oder (eher formell) **infant**. Im Alter von 1–3 Jahren wird ein Baby zum **toddler**, vermutlich weil Kinder in diesem Alter teilweise noch sehr unsicher gehen (**to toddle** *tapsen*).
Niemals darf man über ein Ungeborenes oder ein Baby übrigens als **it** sprechen, was deutschen Muttersprachlern häufig passiert, da es bei uns ja **das Baby** heißt. Über ein Baby im Mutterleib spricht man im Englischen mit **he or she**.

18. Word master

Hoppla, hier ist ja was gründlich schief gegangen. Gelingt es Ihnen, den Text wieder herzustellen?

"Now Darling, **1.** r ____________; don't panic," Bethan

2. q ____________ says.

"Your **3.** w ____________ have broken! Oh **4.** m ____________ God!

We **5.** n ____________ to go to **6.** h ____________, or to my

7. m ____________ house! She's a **8.** m ____________! She knows

9. w ____________ to do!"

"I **10.** k ____________, Darling, but **11.** w ____________ is your

mother's **12.** h ____________?"

Matthew is **13.** a ____________ to hit **14.** h ____________ head

against the **15.** s ____________ wheel again **16.** w ____________

suddenly, in **17.** t ____________ middle of the **18.** s ____________

storm, they **19.** s ____________ a strange **20.** l ____________.

Es gibt viele gute Methoden, seinen Wortschatz zu erweitern. Hören, sehen, bewegen, sich unterhalten – welcher Lerntyp sind Sie? Probieren Sie aus, welche Methode für Sie selbst am besten funktioniert. Sehen Sie sich beispielsweise Ihren Lieblingsfilm auf Englisch mit Untertiteln an, suchen Sie sich eine Vokabel-App aus, die Sie selbst befüllen können, oder digitalisieren Sie neue Vokabeln fürs Handy oder andere Abspielgeräte, damit Sie beispielsweise beim Joggen Wörter lernen können. Oder probieren Sie doch mal, kleine Texte zu schreiben und neue Wörter darin einzubauen. Je witziger der Text, desto leichter kann man sich die Wörter einprägen. Mehr als sieben neue Wörter am Stück sollten es übrigens nicht sein.

19. Grammar master

Jetzt sind Ihre Grammatikkenntnisse gefragt. Im folgenden Text haben Sie immer zwei Varianten zur Wahl. Entscheiden Sie, welche Lösung die richtige ist.

Bethan and Matthew **1. was / were** driving in their car.

It was snowing very **2. hard / hardly**, and they couldn't see anything.

They **3. mightn't / couldn't** call Matthew's mother because the **4. mobile's signal / signal of their mobile** was dead.

Suddenly, Bethan's waters **5. broke / broken**.

Thank God that three **6. mountain bikers / mountain biker's** could help them.

They **7. knew / know** where Matthew's mother lived.

Mit **could**, **may** und **might** kann man angeben, wie wahrscheinlich es ist, das etwas geschieht.

may: etwas formeller als **could**, drückt einen etwas höheren Grad der Wahrscheinlichkeit aus

The mountain bikers may know the way to New Inn.

Die Mountainbikefahrer kennen vielleicht den Weg nach New Inn.

could: drückt auch aus, dass man etwas tun kann (Fähigkeit)

The mountain bikers could know the way to New Inn.

Die Mountainbikefahrer könnten eventuell den Weg nach New Inn kennen.

might: etwas vorsichtiger als **could** und **may**, drückt eine geringere Wahrscheinlichkeit aus

The mountain bikers might know the way to New Inn.

Die Mountainbikefahrer kennen unter Umständen den Weg nach New Inn.

9. The wrong Bag

The sky is not there.

In its place there are a thousand **adverts** on a hundred television screens, a sea of lights that **constantly** move and change. Red, white, blue, green, orange, gold. Red, white, blue, green, orange, gold. They never stop.

And on the television screens there are giant faces, clips from movies, **news headlines**, **commercials** for cars and perfume, chocolate and beer.

The sounds never stop: the **horns** of the big yellow taxis, the music from the bars and the restaurants. And the voices. So many voices. So many, that they are impossible to understand. And so many languages: English, Spanish, Chinese, Italian, German, Portuguese. They all mix together and are little more than noise to an **onlooker**.

But the smells are the worst. One moment it is the **scent** of hotdogs, onions, tomatoes, **fries** or donuts. Delicious smells that make the stomach **rumble**. But then it is cigarettes, alcohol, **garbage** and **vomit**. And all of this mixes with the sweat of the thousands of people in one place.

Jake begins to feel sick again and looks down at his dirty old **sneakers**.

Next to him Nick smiles. "You don't like it here, do you, kid?" he

adverts
- Werbespots
constantly
- ständig

news headlines
- Schlagzeilen
commercials
- Werbespots
horns
- Hupen

onlooker
- Betrachter
scent
- Duft, Geruch
fries
- (AE) Pommes
rumble
- knurren
garbage
- (AE) Abfall
vomit
- Erbrochenes
sneakers
- (AE) Turnschuhe

says. He always calls Jake 'kid', but he must be the same age as him: twelve or thirteen.

"It's okay," Jake says and looks up again. He has to be stronger, he knows; he has to be more like Nick.

"You're just hungry. After we eat, you will think this place is the best in the world. With a full **belly** you can sit and watch this all day."

belly – *Bauch*

"It's just… well, why don't we come at night? Isn't it better at night, Nick?"

"How **dumb** are you?" his new friend says, and he looks **annoyed**. "At night they **worry**. At night everyone worries in New York. In the day, when it's hot and sunny like today, they don't worry about anything. They just watch those big screens, take pictures, eat and drink. They don't even look at us twice."

dumb – *(AE) dumm*
annoyed – *genervt*
worry – *sich sorgen*

And Jake knows that he is right.

"Look. It's easy. You do what I say, no problem." And Nick looks at him for a moment: "You look okay now: these new clothes aren't bad."

The new clothes are not new, Jake knows: not really. Nick steals clothes from the **washing lines** on the backstreets. But they are better than the dirty old jeans and green jacket that are now in a **bin** behind the shop where they sit.

washing lines – *Wäscheleinen*
bin – *Abfalltonne*

"You have to look good, kid. Remember that. You have to look like them," he says. "Then they don't worry. You can get near to them. Be **casual**. Look up at the big screens. It's good if you get a camera out and **pretend** to take some **snaps**, you know? Then, when you get the chance… you do it… you grab a bag. A woman's bag is the best: they have more things in them. But a **guy**'s bag is easier. A guy's bag you can just walk away with. If you get a woman's bag, you sometimes have to run." ▶▷▶

casual – *locker*
pretend – *so tust als ob*
snaps – *Schnappschüsse*
guy – *Typ, Kerl*

1. Out in the street

Haben Sie den Text aufmerksam gelesen? Beantworten Sie dann die folgenden Fragen. Mehrere Antworten können richtig sein.

1. What is the situation in the street like?

❍ **A** It's chaotic and busy.
❍ **B** It's ugly.
❍ **C** It's lonely.

2. How old is Jake?

❍ **A** He is 21.
❍ **B** He is 18.
❍ **C** He is about 13.

3. Why don't they go out at night?

❍ **A** People worry.
❍ **B** They have to be in bed.
❍ **C** Their parents won't allow it.

4. Where did Jake get his clothes?

❍ **A** He bought them.
❍ **B** Nick gave them to him.
❍ **C** He stole them.

5. Why does Jake have to wear casual clothes?

❍ **A** He needs to feel good.
❍ **B** He needs to look like a tourist.
❍ **C** He wants to play outside.

6. What does he have to steal?

❍ **A** A camera.
❍ **B** A mobile phone.
❍ **C** A bag.

2. A touristy look…

Wie sehen Touristen aus? Ordnen Sie die Beschreibungen den Bildern zu.

1

2

3

4

5

6

___ **A** mobile phone

___ **B** sunglasses

___ **C** camera

___ **D** shoulder bag

___ **E** tablet

___ **F** wallet

Wallet oder **purse**? Wo ist da der Unterschied? **Wallet** ist ein Geldbeutel, wie er üblicherweise von Männern verwendet wird. Er ist klein und zum Aufklappen. Man kann auch Brieftasche dazu sagen. Eine **purse** dagegen ist ein Damengeldbeutel und etwas größer.

3. TV, TV, TV

Jake befindet sich in einer belebten Stadt. Er ist umgeben von Werbetafeln und Schaufenstern, in denen Fernseher stehen, auf denen Werbung läuft. Was gehört alles zum Thema Fernsehen? Entwirren Sie den Buchstabensalat. Die Bilder helfen Ihnen dabei.

1

2

3

4

5

___ **A** Werbung ______________________ *(ertsvda)*

___ **B** Fernsehbildschirm ______________________ *(letevisnoi neercs)*

___ **C** Filme ______________________ *(vseimo)*

___ **D** Nachrichten ______________________ *(het nwse)*

___ **E** Fernbedienung ______________________ *(motere locontr)*

Advert ist eine mögliche Kurzform des Worts **advertisement** *(Werbung, Anzeige, Werbespot)*. Häufig findet sich eine noch kürzere Variante: **ad**.

4. A pretty ugly street

Die Straße, in der sich Jake befindet, wird ziemlich genau beschrieben. Suchen Sie die Begriffe im Text und tragen Sie sie ein.

1. What does Jake see? **2.** What does Jake smell? **3.** What does Jake hear?

____________	____________	____________
____________	____________	____________
____________	____________	____________
____________	____________	____________
____________	____________	____________
____________	____________	____________

5. Streetwear

Jake soll sich salopp anziehen. Teilen Sie die Begriffe unten in Businesskleidung und saloppe Straßenkleidung ein (einer der Begriffe passt in beide Kategorien):

shirt • blouse • T-shirt • skirt • suit • jeans • blazer • hoodie

casual clothes	business clothes
____________	____________
____________	____________
____________	____________
____________	____________
____________	____________

Was wird Jake tun? Kann er seinen Auftrag erfüllen?

Jake feels really sick now. The sun is somewhere up there, above the **skyscrapers** of Times Square. And the afternoon is hot. The smells and sounds make a horrible mixture.

skyscraper - *Wolkenkratzer*

He thinks about home for a moment, but that is too far away now, and too long ago.

"You want to eat don't you, kid?"

Jake nods.

"And you remember where the cameras are? The **NYPD** ones? The others are nothing. But don't let the NYPD ones see you, or you're not coming back here, not with me."

NYPD - *Polizei von New York*

Jake nods again.

"So we do it now, and we meet back on Ninth Avenue. You got it?" Nick says.

They both stand up, but before Nick moves into the **crowds**, Jake stops him. "But what if someone sees me? What if they stop me?"

crowds - *Menschenmengen*

Nick smiles. "**No worries**. Just say it's the wrong bag."

no worries - *Keine Sorge!*

And then he goes, and Jake is alone.

He moves out into the crowds of people.

He knows where he has to go: to the red stairs.

He moves slowly. No one really sees him;

no one really looks. But he sees, he looks, he watches.

He sees kids his own age laughing and joking.

He looks at the food on the small tables in front of the cafes and bars.

He sees two policemen in the **distance** and he moves the other way. Walking between families and **couples**, businessmen and tourists.

distance - *Entfernung*

couples - *Pärchen (Mehrzahl)*

reaches - *erreicht*
sweaty - *verschwitzt*

When he **reaches** the red steps, he is hot and **sweaty**. Hungry too. But you can't think about that, he tells himself.

He needs to think clearly now. He needs to think like Nick.

On the red steps there is a group of maybe thirty Japanese tourists. They all have a camera and are all taking photos. But their bags are on their shoulders, and there are too many of them, he knows. Most do not see anything, but one always sees something, and one is enough.

So who?

And then he sees the man.

He looks like any other foreign tourist. He has a camera around his neck. Sunglasses on his face. And a map in his hand.

in fact - *eigentlich*
occasionally - *gelegentlich*

Except, Jake is not sure he is a tourist. There is something different about him. The man does not use the camera and does not look at the map. **In fact**, the man does nothing at all. **Occasionally** he just looks at his watch.

But the bag is by his feet. It looks expensive, made from black leather. Nick calls them weekend bags; he says they are the best. Inside them there are wallets, phones, tablets, everything.

Okay. Okay, you can do this, Jake tells himself.

He just needs to be quick. The man never even looks at the bag. So Jake begins to move in his direction, casually. He looks up at the lights and the television screens.

Then he is near enough, and he looks at the man. He thinks again that he is a strange tourist. From here Jake can see that he looks nervous.

grabs - *packt*
expects - *erwartet*
notices - *bemerkt*

But then the man looks to the right, and Jake knows it is his best chance. He **grabs** the bag and moves away. He **expects** to hear a shout, but there is nothing. So he moves into the crowds like Nick does. He wants to run, but he walks and **notices** that the bag is heavy, really heavy. And he begins **to imagine** Nick's face when he sees the bag, and he already begins to imagine the food that he can buy.

to imagine - *sich vorzustellen*

But the bag is heavy, he thinks again. So heavy.

And he slows. Maybe he should look inside, he thinks, just **to make sure**.

to make sure - *um sich zu vergewissern*

He looks around and steps into the **doorway** of a shop for a moment. Then he **kneels down** and opens the bag.

doorway - *Eingang*

kneels down - *kniet sich hin*

And for a moment he does not understand.

There is no **wallet**. No phone, no tablet, no clothes.

wallet - *(AE) Geldbeutel*

There is only…

Then he hears the man shout, and he looks up and sees his angry face running towards him through the crowd.

He has no time to think, but he must. Can he leave the bag? Can he just run away?

Run away? When he knows what the man is going to do?

No. Not this time.

And then he is up and runs too, and he has the bag in his hands.

For a moment he has no idea what to do or where to go. He thinks that maybe Nick would know, that Nick would have some **advice**.

advice - *Ratschlag*

And then he realizes that he does know.

And you remember where the cameras are? The NYPD ones?

Yes, I remember, Jake thinks. But can he get there before the man catches him?

There is another shout from behind him, but Jake keeps moving.

6. The bag

Haben Sie den Text aufmerksam gelesen? Beantworten Sie dann die folgenden Fragen. Mehrere Antworten können richtig sein.

1. Why does Jake have to be careful?

- ❍ **A** The cameras mustn't see him.
- ❍ **B** No one must see him.
- ❍ **C** Nick mustn't see him.

2. How does he feel when he reaches the steps?

- ❍ **A** Tired, fed up, exhausted.
- ❍ **B** Angry, worried, lost.
- ❍ **C** Hot, sweaty, hungry.

3. Why is the man different from the other tourists?

- ❍ **A** He doesn't have a camera.
- ❍ **B** He frequently looks at his watch.
- ❍ **C** He doesn't have a map.

4. What does the stranger look like?

- ❍ **A** He has a scar on his face.
- ❍ **B** He looks like any other tourist.
- ❍ **C** He has a funny hairstyle.

5. Why does Jake choose the bag?

- ❍ **A** It looks expensive.
- ❍ **B** It's easy to get.
- ❍ **C** It was forgotten in the street.

6. Does Jake realize what is in the bag?

- ❍ **A** Yes.
- ❍ **B** No.

Jake ist in New York. Er ist in der 9th Avenue mitten in Manhattan. Kein Wunder also, dass die Stadt so hektisch ist und dass es so viele Wolkenkratzer gibt - schließlich leben über 8 Millionen Menschen hier. Der höchste Wolkenkratzer in New York ist übrigens das One World Trade Center mit 541 Meter gefolgt vom 432 Park Avenue, das 425 Meter hoch ist. Somit ist das berühmte Empire State Building mit 381 Metern auf Platz drei.

7. The people of New York

Wen findet man alles in den Straßen von New York? Lesen Sie noch einmal nach und ordnen Sie die Begriffe den Bildern zu.

1

2

3

4

5

6

___ **A** business people ___ **B** couples ___ **C** NYPD officers

___ **D** ordinary people ___ **E** tourists ___ **F** families

people vs. **peoples**
People ist ein Pluralwort, d. h. es beschreibt eine Mehrzahl *(Leute)*.
Die Einzahl von **people** ist **person** – **one person, two persons, three people**.
Aufgepasst: **peoples** sind *Völker*!

8. Kleine Wörter

Ergänzen Sie den Text und setzen Sie die Wörter sinnvoll ein.
Tipp: Manchmal gibt es mehrere Möglichkeiten.

simply • but • where • again • then

He thinks about home for a moment, **1.** ____________ that is too far away now. He knows **2.** ____________ he has to go. Nick has told him: "No worries. **3.** ____________ say it's the wrong bag." Then he sees the man again. He thinks **4.** ____________ that he is a strange tourist. Something about him is odd. **5.** ____________ he hears the man shout and he knows that it's time for him to run.

9. Wortstellung

Adverbien müssen je nach Art an einer anderen Stelle im Satz stehen.
Adverbien der Art und Weise (**slowly, carefully, simply**) stehen meist hinter dem direkten Objekt (wen/was?), können aber auch vor dem Verb stehen:
Jake looked around the street carefully. / He carefully looked ...
Jake sah sich auf der Straße vorsichtig um.
Adverbien des Ortes (**here, there, next to**) stehen hinter dem direkten Objekt (wen/was?) oder Verb:
Jake stood next to the tourist. *Jake stand in der Nähe des Touristen.*
Adverbien der Zeit (**now, then, yesterday**) stehen am Satzende oder am Satzanfang, wenn sie betont werden.
Now, he was nervous. / He was nervous now. *Jetzt war er nervös. / Er war nervös jetzt.*
Adverbien der Häufigkeit (**often, always, never**) stehen vor dem Vollverb: **Jake often looked around.** *Jake sah sich oft um.*
Das Adverb steht allerdings dahinter, wenn es sich um eine Form von **to be** handelt:
He was always nervous. *Er war immer nervös.*

Bringen Sie jetzt die Satzteile in die richtige Reihenfolge.
Manchmal gibt es zwei Möglichkeiten:

1. was / Jake / yesterday / very nervous /.

____

2. towards / the crowd / moved / slowly / he /.

____

3. to think / back then / needed / he /.

____

4. carefully / wanted / to take / the bag / he /.

____

5. When he had stolen the bag... / looked / he / around / often.

____

Aufgepasst: Ein Adverb darf nie zwischen Verb und Objekt stehen!
He took the bag quickly. oder **He quickly took the bag.**
Im Beispielsatz darf **quickly** also nicht zwischen **took** und **the bag** stehen.

Enthält ein Satz mehrere Adverbien, erscheinen sie in der Regel wie folgt nacheinander:

Art und Weise vor Ort vor Zeit

The police arrived there quickly. (Ort vor Zeit)

He is walking slowly now. (Art und Weise vor Zeit)

He looked carefully inside after finding a quiet place.
(Art und Weise vor Ort vor Zeit)

Diese Regel schließt nicht aus, dass einzelne Adverbien zur Betonung an den Satzanfang vorgezogen werden:

Next, he opened the bag very slowly.

Wie wird das Ganze enden? Ob Jake wohl vom NYPD geschnappt wird?

▶▷▶ Above the crowd he can see the NYPD camera on top of a tall post, and he pushes past the tourists to reach it. For a moment there are people all around him, and he thinks he will never get there, but then he pushes past some kids who shout at him, and he is there. Directly below the camera.

And now? Now what?

He hears another shout, and knows that the man is nearly here, but the camera is not looking at him. It is turning slowly in the other direction.

"Hey!" he shouts, and he begins to jump up and down. "Down here! Look down here!" but he has no idea if anyone can hear him. He opens the bag for everyone to see, and there is a **cry** from a woman near to him, followed by another and another. This must be why the camera turns. Jake holds up the bag, but he is **scared**, so scared, though he has to do it.

cry - *Schrei*

scared - *verängstigt*

"That's mine," the man's voice says behind him. And there are more cries from the crowd, and everyone seems to know what is happening now. "Give it to me," the man says.

Jake looks at the bag one more time. What he sees inside looks just like from the movies: the clock, the **wires** and the heavy packs of something horrible and dangerous. Jake wants to give it to the man because he is so scared.

wires - *Drähte*

But he will not. "No," he answers.

Then someone in the crowd says something, and the man looks around. The scared cries now become angry **shouts**.

shouts - *laute Rufe*

Jake is pushed and he falls and loses the bag. He thinks that the people are shouting at him, and he wants to explain. But it was not the man who pushed Jake and took the bag: it was a policeman;

the man is **underneath** four NYPD officers.

underneath
- *unter*

Jake now realizes that the crowd is not shouting.

It is cheering.

And a police officer helps him to stand and says something about him being a hero. "How did you know, kid?" a voice says, but this time it is not Nick.

"I… I… I didn't," he manages to say. "It's just… it's just the wrong bag."

10. The wrong bag

Haben Sie den Text aufmerksam gelesen? Beantworten Sie dann die folgenden Fragen. Mehrere Antworten können richtig sein.

1. How does Jake get below the camera?

❍ **A** He pushes past some kids.
❍ **B** He pushes past some tourists.
❍ **C** He pushes past the NYPD.

2. Who suddenly talks to Jake?

❍ **A** A man.
❍ **B** A woman.
❍ **C** The police.

3. What is inside the bag?

❍ **A** Books.
❍ **B** Clothes.
❍ **C** A bomb.

4. What happens to the man?

❍ **A** He runs away with the bag.
❍ **B** He is arrested by the police.
❍ **C** He escapes on a bus.

5. What does the crowd do?

❍ **A** They shout at Jake.
❍ **B** They try to catch Jake.
❍ **C** They cheer at Jake.

6. What do the police do with Jake?

❍ **A** They arrest him, too.
❍ **B** They are proud of him.
❍ **C** They are angry with him.

11. Let's put the whole story together

Haben Sie den zweiten Teil grob verstanden? Dann testen Sie es mal. Kreuzen Sie an, ob folgende Aussagen richtig oder falsch sind.

	RIGHT	WRONG
1. Jake is an adult in New York.	❍	❍
2. He is an experienced thief.	❍	❍
3. He steals a bag from a man.	❍	❍
4. The police want to arrest Jake.	❍	❍
5. It's actually good that Jake has stolen that bag.	❍	❍

12. Who vs. which

Setzen Sie die passenden Relativpronomen ein:

But it was not the man who pushed Jake...
Aber es war nicht der Mann, der Jake stieß...

Jake is a kid **1.** ____________ lives in New York. He has to pass a test **2.** ____________ is very difficult. But Jake no longer has a dog **3.** ____________ can help him with his job. The dog often distracted the police, **4.** ____________ aren't Jake's friends. He had named his dog Barker. That was a nice name and Barker, **5.** ____________ barked a lot, even listened to the name. Unfortunately, Barker ran away.

Wenn man sich auf etwas oder jemanden bezieht, verwendet man für Personen **who**, für Dinge **which**. Bei Haustieren sagt man **which**, solange die Tiere keinen Namen haben, danach verwendet man **who**.

13. Relativsätze mit / ohne Komma

Bei den Relativpronomen muss man unterscheiden, ob sie entbehrlich oder unentbehrlich sind.

Entbehrliche Relativsätze sind eingeschoben und können im Zweifelsfall weggelassen werden, da der Satz auch ohne sie verständlich ist. Sie werden durch Kommas eingeschlossen:

Jake, who lives in New York, has to steal a bag.

Jake, der in New York lebt, muss eine Tasche stehlen.

Unentbehrliche Relativsätze sind für den Sinn des Satzes notwendig:

Jake pushes past some kids who shout at him.

Jake schubst einige Kinder, die ihn anschreien, zur Seite.

In diesem Fall steht kein Komma.

Setzen Sie bei den folgenden Sätzen da Kommas, wo sie nötig sind.

1. Do you know the boy who steals the bag?
2. The NYPD which is the police in New York are chasing a man.
3. Jake who has no idea what is inside the bag runs away.
4. The bag which he has stolen is the wrong bag.
5. It was not the man who pushed Jake, but the police.
6. Now Jake who is actually a thief is a hero.

14. Relativsätze

Hier ist dem Reporter die Luft ausgegangen, als er über Jakes Heldentat berichtete. Verbinden Sie zwei Sätze mithilfe eines Relativpronomens *(who / which)* so, dass die Sätze besser klingen.

1. Jake is a hero. He is a young boy.

____

2. He stole a bag. In the bag was a bomb.

____

3. He ran away from the man. The man wanted his bag back.

____

4. The police pushed the man to the ground. The man was a terrorist.

____

15. Word master

Hier hat sich der Lückenteufel eingeschlichen. Können Sie ihn trotzdem vervollständigen? Die Übersetzungen hinter der Lücke helfen Ihnen.

Jack is not **1.** s________ *(sicher)* that the man is **2.** r________ *(wirklich)* a tourist, because something is **3.** d________ *(anders)* about him. The man **4.** h________ *(hat)* a camera and a **5.** m________ *(Karte)*, but he isn't **6.** u________ *(benutzen)* either of them. In fact, the **7.** o________ *(einzige)* thing the man is **8.** d________ *(tut)* is looking at his **9.** w________ *(Uhr)* occasionally. Additionally, the bag **10.** b________ *(bei)* the man's feet **11.** l________ *(aussehen)* expensive. It's **12.** m________ *(gemacht)* from black **13.** l________ *(Leder)*. Jack knows **14.** t________ *(dass)* he needs to be **15.** q________ *(schnell)*, although the man **16.** n________ *(nie)* even looks at the **17.** b________ *(Tasche)*.

16. Grammar master

Jetzt sind Ihre Grammatikkenntnisse gefragt. Im folgenden Text stehen immer zwei Varianten zur Wahl und Sie müssen entscheiden, welche Lösung die richtige ist.

Jack **1. slowly / slow** approached the man.
He **2. grabbed / has grabbed** the bag and **3. ran / has run** away with it.
4. If / When he looked inside, he saw that something **5. was / were** wrong.
There was no money inside the bag, but **6. any / some** strange wires.
He **7. have / has** no time to think, but he **8. must / may**.
Can he **9. leaves / leave** the bag?
Can he just **10. run / ran** away?

Aus Jake wurde am Ende ein Held.
Weniger heldenhaft ist diese kleine Anekdote:
Ende des Jahres 2016 ereignete sich ein dreister Diebstahl in Manhattan, einem Stadtteil von New York. Ein Mann stahl am helllichten Tag einen schwarzen Eimer aus einem Lieferwagen - klingt bislang weder dreist noch spektakulär, oder? Der Clou: In dem Eimer befand sich Gold im Wert von 1,6 Millionen Euro. Bislang konnte das Gold nicht gefunden werden.

17. NYPD

Wäre Jake ein normaler Passant, der die Tasche gefunden hätte, würde er diesen Fund auf jeden Fall der Polizei melden. Wie würde dieses Gespräch aussehen? Ordnen Sie die passenden Antworten den Fragen zu und bringen Sie sie anschließend in die richtige Reihenfolge.

1. Hello, NYPD. Why are you calling?

2. Have you seen anyone holding the bag or near it?

3. What is the nature of the object?

4. Are there any other suspects?

5. What is the location of the suspicious bag?

6. What's your name?

- **A** Jake.
- **B** Yes, there is a man who looks like any other foreign tourist. He has a camera around his neck. Sunglasses on his face. And a map in his hand.
- **C** I want to report bag with a suspicious object inside.
- **D** I think it's a bomb.
- **E** He is the only one I can see. But he's talking to someone on the phone.
- **F** Between Times Square and Ninth Avenue.

Richtige Reihenfolge: ______________________________

Das **NYPD** (New York Police Department) ist die kommunale Polizeibehörde der Stadt New York. Ein **NYPD Police Officer** trägt dunkelblaue Hosen und T-Shirt und eine Krawatte. Höhere Dienstgrade tragen ein weißes T-Shirt. Für einen Notruf wählt man in den USA **911**, in Großbritannien 999.

10. Case Closed

Normally Nick likes his job, but not today. Today he just wants to get out of the hot **courtroom**, away from the **serious lawyers** in their black **gowns** and white **wigs** and go and enjoy the sun.

It is a good job, he thinks. It is better than serving drinks in a pub or helping out at his dad's office, but only if it is a short day, and only if the case is closed quickly. But today it is nearly three, and the case is nowhere near closed.

Still, he likes the title of his job. "**Court reporter**" sounds good; it sounds important, and that is exactly how he describes it to any girl that asks. In reality, however, all he does is press 'play' on the **recording device** and write down a few notes about when the **judge** enters, when the **prosecution** or **defence** speaks, or what the final **verdict** is.

And sometimes the **cases** are interesting, and he likes having some good stories to tell the guys in the pub. He also enjoys deciding who is **innocent** and who is **guilty**, but today that is too easy.

So he looks out of the window and waits for the judge. Sometimes he looks across at the **defendant's** sister, a young woman with long, dark hair and sad eyes. But only sometimes, because the defendant and the rest of her family, the Lee family, are wild, and he does not want to make her, or them, angry. They have a

courtroom – *Gerichtssaal*
serious lawyers – *ernste Anwälte*
gowns – *Talare*
wigs – *Perücken*
court reporter – *Gerichts-protokollant*
recording device – *Aufnahmegerät*
judge – *Richter/in*
prosecution – *Staatsanwalt-schaft*
defence – *Verteidigung*
verdict – *Urteilsspruch*
cases – *Fälle*
innocent – *unschuldig*
guilty – *schuldig*
defendant – *Angeklagte/r*

reputation
- *verängstigt*

terrible **reputation** in Bristol, and there is not one of them that does not scare Nick.

All rise
- *Erheben Sie sich*
court clerk
- *Gerichtsdiener/in*
lawyers
- *Anwälte*

"**All rise**!" the **court clerk** says, and the jury, the **lawyers** and the family of the defendant all stand. Nick does too, and he remembers to press the button on the device. He forgot to do it once, and they refused to pay him for the day.

brief
- *kurz*

"Please be seated!" says the judge, a woman of about forty years of age with a serious face and tone. "My summary of this case is **brief**. The jury knows all the details. On Wednesday the fifth of January Mrs Dawson went to the house of her sister, the defendant, Miss Lee. Mrs Dawson was bleeding from her nose and mouth; she also had **marks** on her face. She says her husband, the **deceased** Mr Dawson, hit her there **several** times. There are pictures of these **injuries**, but there is no **proof** that Mr Dawson hit Mrs Dawson. However, that is not why you are here. You are here because when Miss Lee saw her younger sister, she took a pair of scissors from her kitchen table, said something to her sister and left the house. The words she said were 'I will kill him,' but the defendant says she does not remember that. Several people saw the defendant walking around Bristol looking for Mr Dawson. She stopped twice: once at the house of one of Mrs Dawson's friends and once at a local pub. Both times she had the scissors with her, and both times **witnesses testified** that she said 'I will kill him.'

marks
- *Male*
deceased
- *verstorben*
several
- *mehrere, einige*
injuries
- *Verletzungen*
proof
- *Beweis*

witnesses
- *Zeug(inn)en*
testified
- *sagten aus*

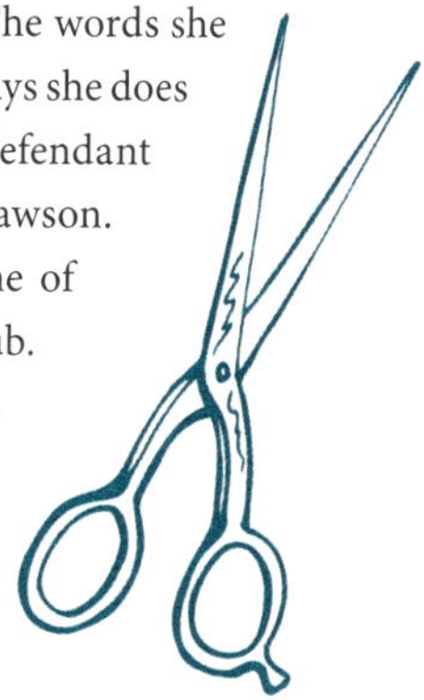

At half past two in the afternoon on the fifth of January Miss Stella Lee found Mr Dawson. He was leaving a cafe with a friend. The friend, Mr Harris, says that Miss Lee did not say anything to Mr Dawson and that the only thing Mr Dawson said was 'Hello'. Miss Lee then **stabbed** Mr Dawson in the neck with the scissors, and he died in seconds **due to loss** of blood. Miss Lee waited until the police came and was arrested. ▶▷▶

stabbed – *stach*
due to – *infolge*
loss – *Verlust*

1. A hot day in court

Haben Sie den Text aufmerksam gelesen? Beantworten Sie dann die folgenden Fragen. Mehrere Antworten können richtig sein.

1. Why is Nick's job so strenuous *(anstrengend)* today?
- ❍ **A** It's hot outside.
- ❍ **B** The case is boring.
- ❍ **C** He didn't sleep well last night.

2. What is his job at court?
- ❍ **A** He is a judge.
- ❍ **B** He is the court clerk.
- ❍ **C** He is the court reporter.

3. What does Nick think about the Lee family?
- ❍ **A** He thinks they are guilty.
- ❍ **B** He thinks they are wild.
- ❍ **C** He thinks they are very nice.

4. What happened once when he forgot to press the recording button?
- ❍ **A** The judge lost the case.
- ❍ **B** He was fired.
- ❍ **C** He didn't get paid for the day.

5. Who is the judge?
- ❍ **A** An old lady.
- ❍ **B** A middle-aged woman.
- ❍ **C** A young man.

6. How did Mr Dawson die?
- ❍ **A** He was run over by a car.
- ❍ **B** He was stabbed violently with a pair of scissors.
- ❍ **C** He was poisoned *(vergiftet)*.

2. In the courtroom

In der Geschichte bei Gericht gab es viele spezielle Wörter. Können Sie die englischen Bezeichnungen den deutschen zuordnen?

1. Richter	**A** defence
2. Gericht	**B** judge
3. Zeuge	**C** lawyer
4. Gerichtssaal	**D** court clerk
5. Anwalt	**E** court reporter
6. Verteidiger	**F** witness
7. Gerichtsschreiber	**G** courthouse
8. Gerichtsdiener	**H** courtroom

Können Sie nun die Beschreibungen den englischen Begriffen zuordnen? Schreiben Sie den Buchstaben von oben zur Beschreibung.

___ **1.** the room in which the trial *(Prozess)* is held

___ **2.** a person who has seen the crime

___ **3.** the person who has to decide in the end whether the person on trial is guilty *(schuldig)* or innocent *(unschuldig)*

___ **4.** the side of the courtroom which tries to convince the jury that the person on trial is innocent

___ **5.** an officer who works at court and e. g. administers the oaths *(Eid)* of witnesses

___ **6.** a person who represents clients in a court or advises them in other legal matters

___ **7.** a person who works at court and writes down or records exactly what is said during a trial

___ **8.** the building in which the trial is held

3. The judge

Was braucht ein guter Richter alles? Ordnen Sie die Beschreibungen den Bildern zu.

__ A gown __ B court hammer

__ C wig __ D code of law

Warum tragen Richter in Großbritannien eigentlich eine Perücke? Bestimmt nicht, weil Pferdehaar so angenehm ist. Die Tradition der Perücke ist bereits über 300 Jahre alt und stammt ursprünglich aus Frankreich. Damals galt der Spruch „Kleider machen Leute" – es war also zum einen ein Ausdruck von Würde und Ansehen. Aber das ist nicht alles. Perücken dienen auch dazu, dem Träger eine gewisse Anonymität zu verleihen und ihn so zu schützen.
Übrigens beginnt diese Tradition allmählich zu bröckeln. Am Zivilgericht tragen Richter mittlerweile keine Perücken mehr. Aber das Strafgericht bleibt dieser Tradition nach wie vor treu.

4. Die Wiederholungszahlen

Wenn man ausdrücken will, dass man etwas mehrmals gemacht hat, gibt es zwei Möglichkeiten. Ist die Anzahl der Wiederholungen unbekannt oder unwichtig, sagt man:
I've done that several times. Will man aber genauer werden, braucht man folgende Zahlen:

1 × **once**

2 × **twice (= two times)**

3 × **three times**

4 × **four times**

She stopped twice: once at the house of one of Mrs Dawson's friends and once at a local pub.

Sie machte zweimal Halt: einmal beim Haus von einem von Frau Dawsons Freunden und einmal bei einer nahen Kneipe.

Füllen Sie jetzt die Lücken im Text mit den passenden Begriffen.

Nick didn't look at the Lees **1.** ____________________ *(einmal)*. Instead he looked at his watch **2.** ____________________ *(mehrmals)*, because it was so hot and he wanted to go home. **3.** ____________________ *(zweimal)* he had thought that the judge would send them home for the day, but now they had to wait for the jury to decide. He knew cases where the jury had not been able to come to a decision and the judge had sent them back to think about it **4.** ____________________ *(fünfmal)*.

Dazu gibt es ein passendes Sprichwort:
Once bitten, twice shy.
Haben Sie eine Idee, wie die deutsche Entsprechung lauten könnte?

5. ____________________

5. Once vs. ones

Once bedeutet **one time**, also *einmal* oder auch *einst(mals)*:
I'll say it once, not twice. *Ich werde es (nur) einmal, nicht zweimal sagen.*
Once upon a time there was a girl named Rapunzel. *Es war einmal ein Mädchen namens Rapunzel.*
Ones dagegen ist der Plural des Pronomens **one**:
This case reminds me of the ones I saw on TV the other day.
Dieser Fall erinnert mich an die, die ich neulich im Fernsehen gesehen habe.

Welches der beiden Wörter ist jeweils das richtige in folgendem Text?

1. ____________ upon a time there were some court cases in the US which were very similar to this one. This case reminds me very much of the **2.** ____________ I read about in the newspapers. **3.** ____________ I told my boss about it, and he told me that he had also followed these cases on TV.

6. One vs. ones

This time, the judge was really strict. He was a very strict one.
The judges Nick had previously experienced were not as strict.
They were very lenient *(nachsichtig)* **ones.**

One und ones wird verwendet, wenn man das **1.** ____________ nicht noch einmal benennen will. **2.** ____________ verwendet man für den Singular, **3.** ____________ für den Plural.

Setzen Sie nun jeweils die passende Form des Pronomens ein.

The families of the victim were present in the courtroom. The **4.** ____________ on the left belonged to Miss Lee, the other **5.** ____________ to Mr Dawson. He didn't like any of them. They weren't as nice as the **6.** ____________ he had seen in other court cases.

7. Verben mit -ing

... he likes having some good stories to tell the guys in the pub.

...er hat gern ein paar gute Geschichten auf Lager, die er den Jungs in der Kneipe erzählen kann.

Im Englischen gibt es Verben, nach denen die **-ing-Form** stehen muss. Man sagt, diese Verben ziehen ein **Gerund** nach sich.

Durch die **-ing-Form** kann grundsätzlich aus einem Verb ein Substantiv gemacht werden:

I like swimming. *Ich mag das Schwimmen.*

Dadurch kann die **-ing-Form (Gerund)** auch verwendet werden, um einen **that**-Satz zu verkürzen:

Nick enjoys it that he can watch the case.

> Nick enjoys watching the case.

Wandeln Sie die folgenden beiden Sätze in Sätze mit Gerund um.

1. Nick dislikes it that he has to sit in a hot room.

____

2. He doesn't like it that he works overtime today.

____

Verben, nach denen ein **Gerund** steht, sind oft Verben, die eine Vorliebe oder eine Abneigung ausdrücken, z. B.: **like, love, enjoy, feel like, hate, dislike, not like, can't stand** oder Verben wie **go, finish, imagine, miss, risk, discuss, give up, mind** *(etwas dagegen haben)*, **practise, recommend** *(empfehlen)*, **suggest** *(vorschlagen)*, **report** *(berichten, aussagen)*.

Nick feels like having a break. *Nick hat Lust, eine Pause zu machen.*

He can't stand working overtime in this heat. *Er kann es nicht leiden, in dieser Hitze Überstunden zu machen.*

Let's go shopping! *Lass(t) uns einkaufen gehen!*

She gave up smoking last week. *Sie hat letzte Woche das Rauchen aufgegeben.*

Nick can't imagine killing someone. *Nick kann es sich nicht vorstellen, jemanden zu töten.*

Ein ganz schön blutiger Mord. Lesen Sie, wie die Verhandlung weitergeht ...

Ladies and gentleman of the jury, you must decide only one thing. The defence says that this is not **murder**, but **manslaughter**. They say this is the case because Miss Lee was not in a **sane** state of mind when she killed Mr Dawson; they say that this crime was **in defence of** her sister. The prosecution says this is not true. They say this is **premeditated** murder because for half an hour Miss Lee looked for Mr Dawson; they also say she made her **intention** clear on three different **occasions**. Please, leave us now, and take some time to **consider** these events."

"All rise!" the court clerk says again. The judge leaves, the jury returns to its room **to make a verdict**, and the Lee family exit to wait in the lobby.

Nick sighs. It is **obvious** what the decision will be, but it looks like he will be here until four now. Cigarette time then, he thinks, and he leaves the courtroom. He has at least ten minutes; no jury can make a decision in less than ten minutes.

He takes the back stairs, passes three or four lawyers in their black gowns and white wigs and feels sorry for them: it is so hot today. Then he pushes open a fire door to his personal smoking area at the back of the court next to the **bins** and lights his cigarette.

The feeling of the sun on his face is good, and the taste of the smoke is even better. Tonight is a good night to go out for a few drinks, he thinks, and he is deciding whom to call, when he hears a female voice. "Yeah, everything is fine, perfect… no, no one has an idea. Not the police, not my **mental** family… of course it will be murder… What? Oh, who cares about her? She'll probably like **prison**, the crazy cow: more people for her to hurt. And then I get his

murder *- Mord*
manslaughter *- Totschlag*
sane *- zurechnungsfähig*
in defence of *- zur Verteidigung*
premeditated *- vorsätzlich*
intention *- Absicht*
occasions *- Gelegenheiten*
consider *- erwägen*
to make a verdict *- ein Urteil fällen*
obvious *- offensichtlich*
bins *- (AE) Mülleimer*
mental *- verrückt*
prison *- Gefängnis*

money, and you and I can get the hell out of this city and out of this country."

Nick walks to the bins and looks around them; on the other side is the sister of the defendant. In the court room she always looks sad and confused. Now, however, she looks only **victorious**.

victorious – *siegreich*

"Jesus," Nick says before he can stop himself, and the girl sees him and closes the **mobile phone** in her hand.

mobile phone – *Handy*

Nick looks at her for a second and then turns and runs back to the door.

He walks back up the stairs feeling confused and uncertain. He has to say something to someone, but who? The judge? Maybe.

He pushes the door to the courtroom open. No one is there. He moves towards another door and then hears someone else enter court.

"Wait," Mrs Dawson says, and she looks like she might cry. "Please wait: I **need to explain**." ▶▷▶

need to explain – *muss etwas erklären*

8. How the story unfolds ...

Der Fall wird allmählich interessant, denn auf einmal ist Miss Lee nicht mehr die Hauptverdächtige. Bringen Sie die weitere Handlung in die richtige Reihenfolge.

A Nick hears a woman who talks on a mobile phone.
B Mrs Dawson, the defendant's sister, wants to talk to him.
C Nick goes outside to smoke a cigarette.
D Nick realizes who the woman on the phone is: the defendant's sister.
E Nick returns to the courtroom.
F The jury needs time to make a decision and leaves the room.
G The woman says on the phone that she has committed the murder.

Richtige Reihenfolge: ______________________

9. Right or wrong?

Haben Sie den zweiten Teil grob verstanden? Dann testen Sie es mal. Kreuzen Sie an, ob folgende Aussagen richtig oder falsch sind.

		RIGHT	WRONG
1.	Nick is very sure that Miss Lee killed the man.	❍	❍
2.	Smoking is not allowed at the courthouse.	❍	❍
3.	Nick overhears a phone call by Miss Lee.	❍	❍
4.	Mrs Dawson threatens Nick.	❍	❍
5.	Nick was not alone when the woman was on the phone. A judge also overheard the phone call.	❍	❍

10. Murder they say...

Miss Lee steht unter Anklage und drei verschiedene Arten von Mord werden erwähnt. Doch was ist was? Ordnen Sie die Definitionen den Straftaten zu:

1. In this case, the person who caused somebody's death did not mean to kill somebody but was negligent *(fahrlässig)* or was drunk or had taken drugs.

2. In this case, the person who caused somebody's death either wanted to kill or hurt the victim severely.

3. In this case, the person who caused somebody's death not only wanted to kill but even planned the murder in advance *(im Voraus)*.

❍ **A** murder *(Mord)*

❍ **B** premeditated murder *(vorsätzlicher Mord)*

❍ **C** manslaughter *(Totschlag)*

11. -ing-Formen

In diesen Sätzen finden sich *-ing*-Formen aller Art. Lesen Sie die Sätze sorgfältig durch und finden Sie für die hervorgehobenen Satzteile eine Übersetzung.

1. Sometimes the job as a court reporter **can be boring**.

2. But now and then, Nick **hears fascinating things** in court.

3. **He likes telling stories** in the pub.

4. **They are waiting** for the jury to come to a decision.

5. He pushes open a fire door to **his personal smoking area**.

6. **The feeling of the sun** on his face is good.

7. Tonight is a good night to go out for a few drinks, he thinks, and **he is deciding** whom to call, when he hears a female voice.

8. **He risks taking a few steps** toward the voice.

9. **The woman sees him looking at her.**

10. He walks back up the stairs **feeling confused** and uncertain.

Was will Mrs Dawson ihm erklären? Was kann Nick, der ja nun die Wahrheit kennt, tun, damit die richtige Person verurteilt wird?

Nick waits. Why not? What can she do to him in here?

She stands near to him, and he can see the tears in her eyes and the **sad expression** on her face, but this time he knows it is not real.

sad expression – *trauriger Gesichtsausdruck*

"I heard you. Your own sister? You wanted her to kill your husband."

"No, you don't understand. I don't know what you heard, but I love my sister, and I used to love my husband."

For a second only Nick waits. Then he shakes his head and is about to turn.

"Look," she says, her voice different now, "I saw you looking at me yesterday. Maybe there is something we can do to make you forget this? Maybe you can take me for a drink." Then she smiles and takes his hand. For a second he does not know what to say, but he knows what to do, and he **pulls his hand away** and moves to the door.

pulls his hand away – *zieht seine Hand weg*

For a second she is silent, but then she speaks again, though this time her voice is hard and angry. "Fine, go and tell them what you heard. Do you have any **proof**? No. So you can tell them what you want, but they can do nothing, and you are still here in Bristol, and so is my family. And they will not like what you say. Do you understand me?"

proof – *Beweis*

Nick stops. He understands, and she is right: there is nothing he can do.

"That's right, little boy. Keep quiet and you are going to be okay. I never hurt anyone; she did. Is it my fault she is so stupid? So easy

manipulate
- *manipulieren*
fake story
- *erfundene Geschichte*

to **manipulate**? A little bit of blood on my face, a few tears, a **fake story** about him hitting me. It was so easy. And if you tell anyone, it is going to be just as easy to finish you. Understand?"

Then the door opens and the lawyers return, and Mrs Dawson's expression of sadness returns. Slowly they all come back in, and Nick knows he has to say something. He has to do something.

savage
- *wild*
violence
- *Gewalt*
defeated
- *besiegt*

But there is no time, and there is nothing he can do. The Lee family is back in the room now, and he looks at them. They are **savage**, terrible people, who love **violence**.

So, he moves back to his desk, and he sits down in the seat and feels **defeated**.

He wants to say something, but without proof he has nothing, and the judge can do nothing.

And he hears the door to the judge's chamber open.

"All rise!" and Nick knows it is too late now.

He stands and is about to press the button on the recording device when he sees the red light flashing.

The red light?

The red light means it is recording.

It is recording…

It was recording…

It recorded…

"Stop!" Nick shouts, and he hands the recording device to the court clerk. "I think the judge needs to listen to this first," he says, and he looks back at the beautiful Mrs Dawson and sees that she is not sad now, and that she is not victorious, and not angry.

suits her best
- *steht ihr am besten*
she is scared
- *sie hat Angst*

And he smiles at her because he thinks this expression **suits her best**.

Yes, he thinks Mrs Dawson looks best when **she is scared**. ■

12. Wie war das nochmal mit den Zeiten?

Nick ist erleichtert, als er sieht, dass sein Aufnahmegerät an ist. Was aber bedeuten diese drei Sätze genau und was wird durch die Zeit, die dabei verwendet wird, jeweils ausgedrückt?

It is recording ...

Die Aufnahme passiert **1.** ______________________.

It was recording ...

Die Aufnahme fand **2.** ______________________ statt,

3. ______________________ Mrs Dawson ihr Geständnis abgab.

It recorded ...

Hier handelt es sich um eine **4.** ______________________, dass die Aufnahme erfolgte.

13. Gegenteile

Im Text finden sich eine Menge Adjektive. Kennen Sie das jeweilige Gegenteil dazu?

1.	sad	**A**	clever
2.	real	**B**	insane, mental
3.	silent	**C**	soft
4.	hard	**D**	tame
5.	angry	**E**	peaceful
6.	stupid	**F**	happy
7.	savage	**G**	loud
8.	sane	**H**	unreal

14. In the news

Mehrere Tage später steht ein Artikel über den Fall in der Zeitung. Setzen Sie die fehlenden Wörter in den Text ein.

stabbed • mobile phone • court room • evidence • who • recording device • recorded • woman • premeditated murder • jury • make a verdict • charged with murder

The case looked hopeless. A young **1.** ____________________ *(Frau)*, Miss Lee, was accused of **2.** ____________________ *(vorsätzlicher Mord)*, because according to evidence (Beweislage) she had **3.** ____________________ *(erstochen)* Mr Dawson with a pair of scissors. The **4.** ____________________ *(Geschworenen)* were about to **5.** ____________________ *(ein Urteil fällen)*, when by coincidence *(Zufall)* the court reporter overheard Mrs Dawson talking on her **6.** ____________________ *(Handy)*. During the phone call, she confessed that it was actually she **7.** ____________________ *(die/welche)* had committed the crime. Back in the **8.** ____________________ *(Gerichtssaal)* she talked to the court reporter and told him that he didn't have any **9.** ____________________ *(Beweis)* against her. Luckily, the **10.** ____________________ *(Aufnahmegerät)* had still been on and had **11.** ____________________ *(aufnehmen)* her confession. So, the case against Miss Lee was closed. Now, Mrs Dawson is **12.** ____________________ *(unter Mordanklage)*.

15. Die Zeiten

Hier wartet ein kunterbunter Zeitenmix auf Sie. Füllen Sie die Lücken aus und achten Sie dabei auf Signalwörter!

simple present (4×) • **present progressive** (4×) • **simple past** (2×)
present perfect (2×) • **Gerund** (1×)

At the moment Nick **1.** ______________ *(sit)* in the court room.
The judge **2.** ______________ *(just, enter)* the room and
3. ______________ *(look)* at the defendant.
"You all may sit down. I **4.** ______________ *(come)* to a
verdict. After you **5.** ______________ *(kill)* Mr Dawson some
weeks ago, you **6.** ______________ *(try)* to trick the jury and
me. I don't like **7.** ______________ *(be)* tricked. This is why
I **8.** ______________ *(sentence)* you to 10 years of prison."
While the judge **9.** ______________ *(talk)* to the defendant,
Nick **10.** ______________ *(look)* at her all the time.
She **11.** ______________ *(not blink)* once. He
12. ______________ *(think)*:
"This **13.** ______________ *(be)* a really cruel woman. I cannot believe
that someone who looks so beautiful can be so brutal."

16. Word master

Hier hat sich wieder der Lückenteufel eingeschlichen. Können Sie den Text wiederherstellen? Die Übersetzungen hinter der Lücke helfen Ihnen.

Nick knows **1.** t__________ *(dass)* he has to say **2.** s__________ *(etwas)* about Mrs Dawson's confession. Although he **3.** d__________ *(mag nicht)* the Lee family – they all look **4.** s__________ *(wild)* and seem to love **5.** v__________ *(Gewalt)*, Nick **6.** k__________ *(weiß)* that he is the **7.** o__________ *(einzige)* one who knows the truth. He **8.** f__________ *(fühlt)* defeated. He has no proof and so the **9.** j__________ *(Richter/in)* can do **10.** n__________ *(nichts)*. Then, however, he **11.** l__________ *(sieht)* at the recording **12.** d__________ *(Gerät)*: the red **13.** l__________ *(Licht)* is flashing. It was recording …

17. Grammar master

Jetzt sind Ihre Grammatikkenntnisse gefragt. Im folgenden Text stehen Ihnen immer zwei Varianten zur Wahl und Sie müssen entscheiden, welche Lösung die richtige ist.

So far, Nick has been desperate. **1. If / when** he only had some proof! Then he **2. see / sees** something: the red light **3. blinks / is blinking**. Nick is **4. real / really** excited when he sees this. **5. Now / No** he knows that he has some proof. **6. Once / Ones** he realises this, he talks to the judge. Mrs Dawson **7. angry / angrily** looks at him.

11. The Best Place

Two months had passed since Lynn and Edward had moved from London into an old house in Evington, and the place was still a **mess**. When their boss had told them that he wanted them to take over his restaurant there, they hadn't been very **enthusiastic** about the offer. Their boss, however, had **emphasized** several times that they were the best couple he could imagine for this role. And, even though it had meant leaving their beloved London, the job was definitely a **promotion**. They were now **in charge of** their own small, but **decent**, restaurant.

mess
- *Durcheinander*
enthusiastic
- *begeistert*
emphasized
- *betont*
promotion
- *Beförderung*
in charge of
- *verantwortlich für*
decent
- *vernünftig*

Once the decision to accept the offer had been made, however, Lynne and Edward knew all too well that they only had a month to move up to Leicester. They had to find a place to live, and they needed to move their furniture and all their other belongings as soon as possible. Luckily enough, Edward almost immediately found an advertisement in a newspaper for a small house which fit their budget. All the other ads that they had discovered had definitely been too expensive. This place, it seemed, was the best that they could afford. It **consisted of** two floors and a small attic, and they would even have a cellar. Lynn liked the large windows and the pointed roof shown in the ad. So, the two signed the **contract** without having seen the house with their own eyes and laughed about **buying this pig in a poke**.

consisted of
- *bestand aus*
contract
- *Vertrag*
buying the pig in a poke
- *die Katze im Sack kaufen*

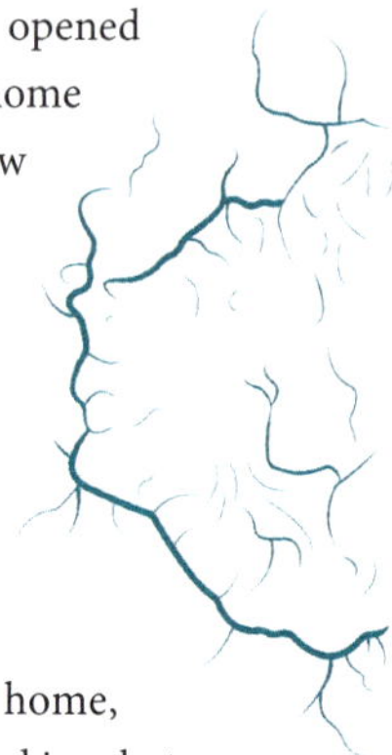

acquired – *erworben*

dilapidated – *herunter-gekommen*

scattered – *verstreut*

DIY-type – *Heimwerker-*

drill – *Bohrer*

to lay parquet – *Parkett zu verlegen*

They stopped laughing when they opened the door of their newly **acquired** home for the first time and realized just how much renovation was necessary. The house was a mess – it was old and **dilapidated**, and not a single room looked the way that they had imagined. Both sighed deeply – and moved in. Ever since, their lives had been very busy. During the day, they had to work in the restaurant, and once they came home, they had to work in the house. Lynn stood in what was going to be their living room and looked around. Wherever she looked, there were tools **scattered** across the floor. They had never really been the **DIY-type** of couple, but after a while, both had actually displayed signs of talent and had learned how to use a hammer, a **drill** and how to **lay parquet**. Still, in the evenings, when they were lying in bed, Lynn thought to herself, "How can this ugly place ever become my home? It's a nightmare." Edward didn't seem to mind, but she was deeply disappointed.

to plaster – *vergipsen*

crack – *Riss*

broomstick – *Besenstiel*

got hold of sth. – *etwas zu fassen bekam*

It was on a Sunday, when Edward, who had just started **to plaster** the holes in the walls, discovered a larger **crack** in one of the walls in their bedroom. When he poked into the crack with a **broomstick** to see how deep it was, he heard a tinny sound. Carefully, he felt around with his fingers for whatever it was that was hidden in there. When he **got hold** of something, he pulled it out and saw that it was a small, flat box.

1. A new place

Haben Sie den Text aufmerksam gelesen? Beantworten Sie dann die folgenden Fragen. Mehrere Antworten können richtig sein.

1. Why did Lynn and Edward move?
- ❍ **A** They lost their old job.
- ❍ **B** They were offered a better job.
- ❍ **C** They didn't like London.

2. Why did they choose this house?
- ❍ **A** Their boss chose it for them.
- ❍ **B** It was all they could afford.
- ❍ **C** It is very close to their work.

3. What do they have to renovate?
- ❍ **A** Basically everything.
- ❍ **B** Nothing: the house is perfect.
- ❍ **C** The attic needs renovating.

4. How is the renovating going on?
- ❍ **A** It's hell. They needed to hire help.
- ❍ **B** It's hell, but they can manage.
- ❍ **C** They stopped renovating.

5. How does Lynn like the house?
- ❍ **A** She loves it.
- ❍ **B** She has come to like it.
- ❍ **C** It's a big disappointment.

6. What does Edward find in the wall?
- ❍ **A** He finds a lot of dirt.
- ❍ **B** He finds an old box.
- ❍ **C** He finds a letter.

Engländer kaufen ihr erstes Haus (oder Wohnung) oft sehr jung und steigen damit unten auf der *Immobilienleiter*, der sog. **property ladder** ein. Im Laufe ihres Lebens verkaufen sie immer wieder ihr Haus bzw. ihre Wohnung und kaufen eine für ihren Lebensabschnitt passende Immobilie.

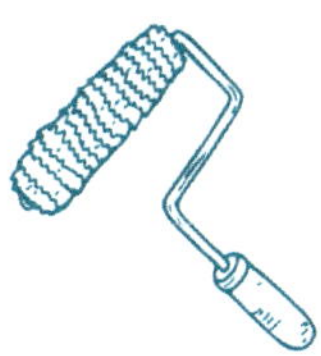

2. The house

Lynn liked the large windows and the pointed roof shown in the ad.

Die großen Fenster und das Spitzdach aus der Annonce gefielen Lynn.

Wie sieht das Haus von Edward und Lynn aus? Ordnen Sie die einzelnen Bilder den Begriffen zu.

1
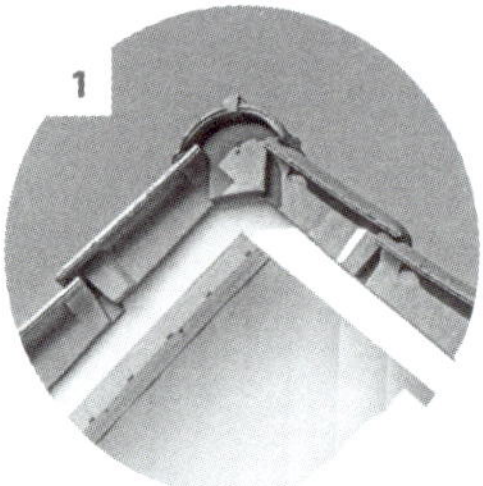

2
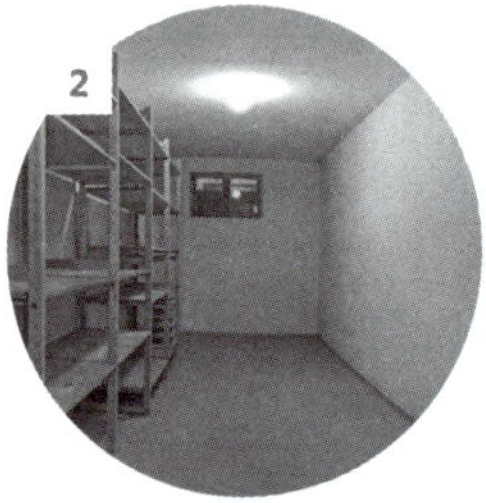

3

4

5

6
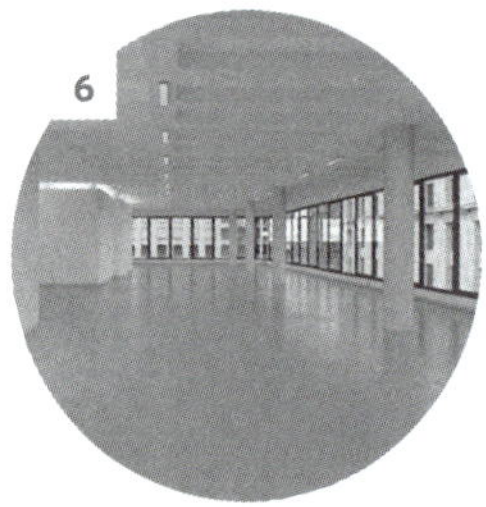

___ **A** large windows

___ **B** doorstep

___ **C** attic

___ **D** floor

___ **E** pointed roof

___ **F** cellar

Je nachdem, in welchem Land sie sich befinden, werden die Etagen anders gezählt. In den USA heißt das Erdgeschoss **first floor**, in Großbritannien sagt man dazu **ground floor**. Der erste Stock ist in den USA entsprechend der **second floor**, während man in Großbritannien **first floor** dazu sagt.

3. The DIY-Couple

DIY ist die Abkürzung für *do it yourself*, also etwas selbst zu machen. Im Laufe der Zeit haben Edward und Lynn gelernt, gut mit Werkzeugen umzugehen. Welche Werkzeuge benötigen sie für die Renovierung? Ordnen Sie die Begriffe den Bildern zu.

1

2

3

4

5

6

___ **A** nails

___ **B** pliers

___ **C** screws

___ **D** drill

___ **E** saw

___ **F** hammer

Für Heimwerker-Freunde ist **B&Q** ein Muss. Die Bauhaus-Kette hat mittlerweile mehr als 350 Filialen und ist damit die größte im Vereinigten Königreich.

4. Proverbs

Der Text enthält ein englisches Sprichwort. Finden Sie es und schreiben Sie es auf.

1. ______________________________

Die Katze im Sack kaufen.

Sehen Sie sich die folgenden englischen Sprichwörter an. Wie lauten die deutschen Pendants dazu? Ordnen Sie zu.

2. A bad workman always blames his tools.

3. A new broom sweeps clean.

4. As thick as a brick.

5. Broken crockery brings you luck.

6. No pain - no gain.

A Ohne Fleiß kein Preis.

B Dumm wie Bohnenstroh.

C Scherben bringen Glück.

D Ein schlechter Handwerker schimpft immer auf sein Werkzeug.

E Neue Besen kehren gut.

Wie heißt die deutsche Entsprechung zu diesem Sprichwort?

Many hands make light work.

7. ______________________________

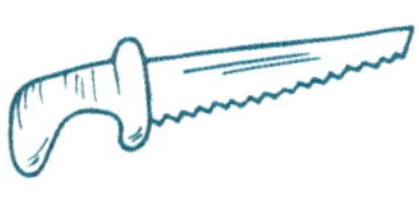

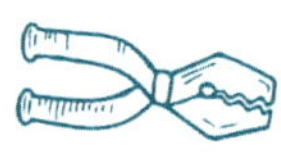

5. Das Past Perfect

Lesen Sie das Zitat und finden Sie die beiden Zeitformen des *past perfect*. Schreiben Sie sie auf.

1. ____________________

2. ____________________

Diese Zeit heißt *past perfect*. Was fällt Ihnen bei der Bildung der Zeit auf? Ergänzen Sie die Regel.

Two months had passed since Lynn and Edward had moved from London into an old house in Evington, and the place was still a mess.

Es waren zwei Monate vergangen, seit Lynn und Edward aus London in ein altes Haus in Evington gezogen waren und das Haus war immer noch ein Chaos.

Das **past perfect** wird gebildet aus:

3. __________ + **4.** __________ + **5.** __________ (bei regelmäßigen Verben) bzw. **6.** __________ Verbform (3. Verbform, **past participle**). Es wird verwendet, wenn man ausdrücken will, dass in der Vergangenheit etwas geschehen ist, bevor etwas anderes sich ereignet hat. Das **past perfect** ist also die Vorvergangenheit.

Entscheiden Sie, in welche der folgenden Lücken das *past perfect* passt, und wann Sie das *simple past* verwenden müssen:

After Edward and Lynn **7.** __________ *(move)* to Evington, they **8.** __________ *(start)* a new job. It was before Edward **9.** __________ *(discover)* the box that Lynn **10.** __________ *(find)* everything very annoying. They **11.** __________ *(have to)* find out who the box belonged to before they **12.** __________ *(can)* go on with their work.

Was befindet sich wohl in dieser Schachtel? Und warum hat man sie in der Mauer versteckt?

"Honey, look what I found in the wall," he called over to Lynn. "What is it?" she **inquired** curiously and wiped her hair from her sweaty forehead.

inquired - fragte nach

"It's a small box. Shall I throw it away, or do you want to check what's inside?" he asked her.

Lynn took the box, blew away a layer of dust and opened it. "Hmm," she **muttered** when she looked inside. She found a small stack of **yellowed** photos, which she then **flipped through**. One showed a young girl of about five in a lovely children's room, and another a young couple in a **neat** living room. In a third picture, you could see the couple again, this time in a beautiful bathroom trying to bathe two children. A final picture had **captured a moment** of intimacy: it showed an elderly couple gently **embracing** each other. This photo had been taken on the doorsteps of… the same house that was now theirs.

muttered - *murmelte*
yellowed - *vergilbt*
flipped through - *blätterte durch*
neat - *(hier): hübsch*
captured a moment - *einen Moment eingefangen*
embracing - *... das sich umarmte*

"Eddy, look. This box must belong to one of the **former** owners. What do you think?"

former - *ehemalig*

Edward nodded. "You know what? I'm tired of working. Why don't we ring at the neighbours' door and find out who that box belongs to!"

Lynn **hugged** Edward enthusiastically. "That's a wonderful idea. That way we also get to know the neighbours and we have a mystery to **solve**."

hugged - *umarmte*
solve - *lösen*

Knocking on their neighbours' doors, the two realized that they had actually moved into a rather **endearing** neighbourhood. Most of their neighbours were elderly people who had lived in their houses for years. But all of them were very nice and helpful and warmly

endearing - *liebenswert*

welcomed Edward and Lynn into their neighbourhood. Best of all, however, was the fact that all of them knew the people in the photos and that everyone had something else that they could say about them. After talking to four different people, Lynn and Edward were able to put together the following story. The man's name was Henry Sinclair, and the woman's was Beth. Henry had died three years ago after a long and loving marriage to Beth. They had raised two children, who by now had families of their own. Beth had lived in the house until recently, but then she had **suffered a stroke**. Even though she had **recovered** from it, she had decided to sell the house – to a man from across the city, who after just a year had sold it on to Lynn and Edward – and move into a home for elderly people. Lynn and Edward's last neighbour, Mr Taylor, finally gave them the address of the **retirement home**.

It was late in the afternoon when Edward and Lynn arrived there. Although it was shortly before supper, **a nurse** let them in. When they asked for Beth Sinclair, they were told to wait in the hall. A few minutes later, a **well-groomed** elderly woman was pushed into the hall in a **wheelchair** by a nurse and was **introduced** as Beth.

"What can I do for you?" she inquired curiously.

"I think we have found something that belongs to you," Lynn said and held out the box.

With **trembling** hands, the old lady took the box from Lynn, gently **patted** her hand and **pressed** the box to her heart.

"I don't know how to thank you," she said, and from the way her voice trembled you could tell that she was deeply touched. "After the stroke, I moved here, but I forgot where I had hidden

suffered a stroke – *einen Schlaganfall erlitten*
recovered – *sich erholt*
retirement home – *Altersheim*
a nurse – *Pfleger(in)*
well-groomed – *gepflegt*
wheelchair – *Rollstuhl*
introduced – *vorgestellt*
trembling – *zitternd*
patted – *streichelte*
pressed – *drückte*

my photos. I knew they had to be somewhere in the house, but you know… my memory is getting a little **rusty**. However, I will always remember that I had such a happy life in my house, first as a child and then with my family."

rusty
- eingerostet

Lynn and Edward looked at Beth Sinclair and then they looked at each other – "I'm sure your house is the best place we could have bought," Lynn **replied** – and she meant it.

replied
- antwortete

6. A treasure in a small box

Haben Sie den Text aufmerksam gelesen? Beantworten Sie dann die folgenden Fragen. Mehrere Antworten können richtig sein.

1. What did Edward find in the wall?
- ❍ **A** He found some money.
- ❍ **B** He found a family of mice.
- ❍ **C** He found an old box.

2. What can be seen in the photos?
- ❍ **A** Beautiful landscapes.
- ❍ **B** Photos of London.
- ❍ **C** A happy family.

3. How do they find Beth's address?
- ❍ **A** It's on the back of one of the photos.
- ❍ **B** They ask the neighbours.
- ❍ **C** They get it out of the telephone book.

4. Where does Beth live now?
- ❍ **A** She lives with her family.
- ❍ **B** She lives in a home for elderly people.
- ❍ **C** She lives with her husband in a newer house.

5. How does Beth react when she sees the photos?
- ❍ **A** She is very happy.
- ❍ **B** She doesn't remember them.
- ❍ **C** She is angry.

6. How does Lynn feel at the end?
- ❍ **A** She wants to go back to London.
- ❍ **B** She starts to like the house.
- ❍ **C** She wants to sell the house.

7. The rooms of a house

Lynn erkennt auf den Fotos viele Räume aus ihrem Haus wieder. Welche Räume gibt es in einem Haus überhaupt? Ordnen Sie die Beschreibungen den Bildern zu:

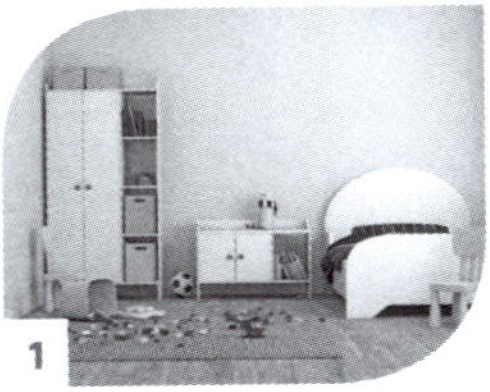
1

2

3

4

5

6

___ **A** kitchen

___ **B** living room

___ **C** bedroom

___ **D** children's room

___ **E** bathroom

___ **F** terrace

Können Sie aus diesem Buchstabensalat noch weitere Räume finden?

7. ______________________

(dralre *Speisekammer*)

8. ______________________

(nidgni ormo *Esszimmer*)

9. ______________________

(tranence moor *Eingangsbereich, Vorraum*)

8. I tell you...

In der Geschichte finden Sie viele Begriffe, die zum Wortfeld *sagen* gehören. Suchen Sie diese Begriffe heraus und tragen Sie sie bei der passenden deutschen Übersetzung ein!

1. ______________________ *nachfragen*

2. ______________________ *fragen*

3. ______________________ *sagen*

4. ______________________ *antworten*

5. ______________________ *murmeln*

Welche der folgenden Substantive passen nun zu welchen der englischen Verben oben? Ordnen Sie auch diese zu.
Tipp: Manche Wörter können mehrfach oder gar nicht vorkommen.

6. inquiry ______________________

7. reply ______________________

8. murmur / mutter ______________________

9. question ______________________

10. response ______________________

Zu diesen Verben gibt es natürlich eine Vielzahl von Wendungen und Sprichwörter **(sayings)**. Hier ein paar ausgewählte zum Verb **to say**:

saying this *mit diesen Worten, hiermit*

Just saying. *Ich mein ja nur.*

That goes without saying. *Das versteht sich von selbst.*

9. In the retirement home

Lynn und Edward besuchen Mrs Sinclair im Altersheim. Welche Begriffe können ihnen dabei begegnen? Ordnen Sie die Bilder den Begriffen zu.

The last neighbour, Mr Taylor, finally gave them the address of the retirement home.

Der letzte Nachbar, Mr Taylor, gab ihnen schließlich die Adresse des Seniorenheims.

1 

2

3 

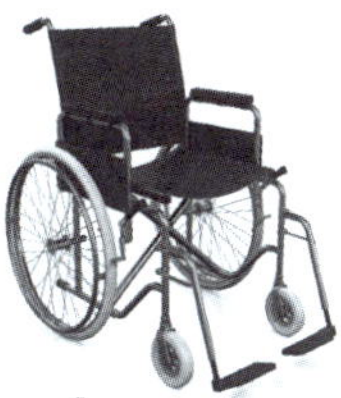
4

5 

6 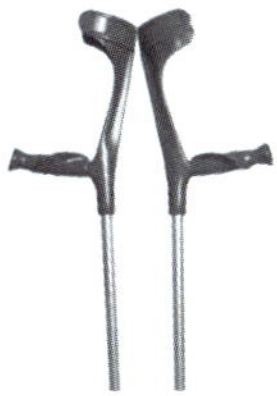

___ **A** wheelchair ___ **B** nurse ___ **C** elderly person

___ **D** crutches ___ **E** walking aid ___ **F** doctor

10. Getting sick

Mrs Sinclair hatte ein langes und erfülltes Leben. Im Alter wurde sie leider krank. Erkennen Sie die Krankheiten und ordnen Sie ihnen die englischen (und deutschen) Begriffe zu.

1. This is a medical condition in which the heart does not get enough blood. This can cause great pain in the left arm, the shoulder or the chest. If not treated instantly, it can end badly.

2. This is a medical condition which affects mostly old people. Symptoms are memory loss and gradually increasing confusion.

3. This medical condition affects the eyes and damages the optic nerve. It can lead to blindness.

4. This is a medical condition where the brain does not get enough oxygen. It can be detected (= *entdeckt*) by sudden loss of speech or paralysis of one side of the body. If not treated instantly, this can end badly.

5. This is a medical progressive disorder. Here, the brain's nerve cells are attacked. The consequences are memory loss or loss of language skills. Behaviour might change as well.

___ **A** stroke *(Schlaganfall)*

___ **B** heart attack *(Herzinfarkt)*

___ **C** Alzheimer's disease *(Alzheimer)*

___ **D** dementia *(Demenz)*

___ **E** glaucoma *(Grüner Star)*

11. The passive voice

Sehen Sie sich das Zitat hier genauer an. Es kommen zwei Passivkonstruktionen darin vor. Notieren Sie die beiden passiven Verbformen.

A few minutes later, a well-groomed elderly woman was pushed into the hall in a wheelchair by a nurse and was introduced as Beth.

Ein paar Minuten später wurde eine sorgfältig zurechtgemachte ältere Frau in einem Rollstuhl von einer Schwester in die Eingangshalle geschoben und als Beth vorgestellt.

1. ____________________

2. ____________________

Das Passiv wird gebildet mit einer Form von:

3. __________ + **4.** ____________ + __________

(bei regelmäßigen Verben) bzw. unregelmäßige Verbform (= 3. Verbform, **Past Participle**).

Wie auch das Aktiv gibt es das Passiv in allen Zeiten.

Wandelt man einen Aktivsatz in einen Passivsatz um, tauschen Subjekt und Objekt den Platz, d.h. das Objekt des Aktivsatzes wird zum Subjekt des Passivsatzes:

They buy a house. > A house is bought.

Sie kaufen ein Haus. > Ein Haus wird gekauft.

Der/die Handelnde kann als **By-Agent** genannt werden:

Edward found a box. It was found by Edward.

Edward fand eine Kiste. Sie wurde von Edward gefunden.

Versuchen Sie es selbst und setzen Sie die folgenden Sätze ins Passiv:

6. Edward and Lynn renovated the house.

____

7. The doctor tells them to wait in the hallway.

____

8. A nurse pushes Mrs Sinclair into the hallway.

____

Wandeln Sie nun die folgenden Sätze in Aktivsätze um:

9. They were given the address by Mr Taylor.

____

10. The woman was introduced as Beth by the nurse.

____

11. The photos were hidden by Beth in the wall.

____

12. If oder when und unless oder whether

Diese Wörter haben ähnliche Bedeutungen, werden aber unterschiedlich eingesetzt. Versuchen Sie es selbst:

if ***(wenn / falls)*** • **when** ***(wenn / sobald)*** •
unless ***(wenn nicht / sofern nicht)*** • **whether** ***(ob / falls)***

I don't know **1.** __________ Lynn would ever have moved to this house **2.** __________ she had seen the place before. **3.** __________ she and Edward moved in, the place was a real mess. **4.** __________ Edward hadn't found the box, they would have surely had an even more miserable time than they did anyway. Lynn would have stayed angry with the house **5.** __________ they had met Beth.

Geschafft!
Das war die letzte Übung des Sprachkurses.
Sie haben sicherlich viel dazu gelernt. Weiterhin
viel Spaß und Erfolg beim Englischlernen.

Lösungen

1 The Stranger

1. A Trip to Whitby
1. A, B, C; **2.** B; **3.** C; **4.** A; **5.** B; **6.** C

2. Travelling Vocabulary
1. E, **2.** A, **3.** B, **4.** C, **5.** F, **6.** D

3. Where are you from?
1. France, **2.** Germany, **3.** United States of America, **4.** Italy, **5.** China, **6.** England

4. To be or not to be
Tabelle: I am, you are, he / she / it is
1. are, **2.** is, **3.** is, **4.** is, **5.** are

5. The End of the Trip
right: 1, 3; wrong: 2, 4, 5

6. Dinge beschreiben
1. polite, **2.** interesting, **3.** thirsty
Adjektive: small, famous, strange, wrong

7. Simple Present
1. -s, **2.** -es, **3.** -es, **4.** -ies

8. Simple Present
1. say, **2.** says, **3.** smile

9. There, their oder they're?
1. There, **2.** they're, **3.** their

10. Verneinung im Simple Present
1. I do not close the curtain, **2.** I do not like,
3. He does not smile
4. I don't see that strange expression in his face. **5.** I don't want to ask him what is so funny. **6.** The stranger doesn't smile.

11. I can't do that
1. We can see the Abbey,
2. I cannot understand

12. What is correct?
1. A, **2.** A, **3.** A, **4.** B, **5.** B

13. My dear friend...
1. his, **2.** my, **3.** His, **4.** his, **5.** our, **6.** your, **7.** his

14. The Stranger
1. B, **2.** C, **3.** A, **4.** E, **5.** F, **6.** D

2 Always be Prepared

1. Ein Pfadfinderausflug
1. C, **2.** B, **3.** B, **4.** B, **5.** C, **6.** A

2. Farben
1. green, **2.** blue, **3.** yellow, **4.** brown, **5.** red,
6. grey
7. white (weiß), **8.** black (schwarz), **9.** orange (orange), **10.** pink / purple (rosa / lila)

3. Eine Landschaft beschreiben
1. wonderful, **2.** impressive, **3.** beautiful,
4. fantastic

4. To be a scout
1. F, **2.** A, **3.** D, **4.** C, **5.** E, **6.** B

5. Objektpronomen
1. us, **2.** him, **3.** me, **4.** them

6. Vorschläge machen
1. Shall, **2.** should; A

7. Die Insel erkunden
1. E, **2.** A, **3.** D, **4.** B, **5.** F, **6.** C

8. The end of the trip
1. wrong, **2.** right, **3.** wrong, **4.** right

9. Das Present Progressive
1. Das Present Progressive bildet man mit einer Form von be + Verb + -ing.
2. is shouting, **3.** are exploring,
4. am speaking **5.** are walking

10. Simple Present oder Present Progressive?
1. walk, **2.** explore, **3.** looks, **4.** is checking,
5. see, **6.** is, **7.** run, **8.** look, **9.** sees, **10.** says,
11. is waving, **12.** are

11. Nationalitäten
1. English, **2.** Dutch, **3.** Swiss, **4.** French,
5. Italian, **6.** American, **7.** Irish, **8.** Scottish,
9. Maltese, **10.** Canadian, **11.** Czech,
12. Russian, **13.** Polish
14. I come from Germany, so I am German.

12. Aufforderungen
1. Hurry up, **2.** Come on, **3.** Follow us
4. Das Verb steht immer in der Grundform, das bedeutet, man braucht keine Endungen.
5. A: Be careful! **6.** B: Read the sign! **7.** C: Look at the watch!, **8.** D: Don't panic! **9.** E: Always be prepared!

3 The White Lady of Castell Coch

1. The Ghost of Castell Coch
1. wrong, **2.** wrong, **3.** right, **4.** wrong,
5. wrong, **6.** right, **7.** right, **8.** wrong

2. False friends – falsche Freunde
1. hiked, **2.** wander, **3.** brochure, **4.** decent,
5. dessert, **6.** prospect(s), **7.** chef, **8.** gift

3. Ein Blick in den Spiegel
1. D, **2.** A, **3.** E, **4.** B, **5.** C
Lösungsbeispiel: I am small. I don't wear braces. I wear glasses.

4. Allein im Wald
1. dark forest, **2.** spooky trees, **3.** pale moon,
4. dark night sky, **5.** small torch

5. Das Simple Past
(1) regelmäßig, (2) unregelmäßig
(3) Grundform des Verbs, (4) -ed
Regelmäßige Verben: dared, stayed, whispered, looked, replied, used, asked, lived, walked, shivered
Unregelmäßigen Verben: was (be), knew (know), said (say), saw (see), went (go), led (lead), began (begin), fell (fall), died (die)

6. The White Lady
1. walked, **2.** wanted, **3.** told, **4.** wore, **5.** lived,
6. were, **7.** felt, **8.** walked

7. Die Steigerungsformen
1. bravest, **2.** younger, taller, **3.** paler, darker,
4. thinner, thinner, **5.** thinner, taller,
6. the most beautiful

8. The Ghost
1. B, **2.** A, **3.** A, **4.** A, **5.** C, **6.** B

9. Terr...
1. terrible, **2.** terrifying;
(3) terrible, (4) terrifying, (5) terrific

10. Was Sie nicht sagen...
1. D, 2 C, **3.** F, **4.** A, **5.** E, **6.** B

11. Past Progressive
1. was hiking, **2.** heard, **3.** turned, **4.** saw,
5. laughed (sie fängt an zu lachen, als Mel sich umdreht) / was laughing (sie lacht schon die ganze Zeit)

12. Possessive 's
1. 's **2.** s' **3.** of **4.** Mel's face was pale.
5. The wall of the castle was old.
6. The girls' torches were bright.

4 A Little Slice of Heaven

1. The First Encounter
1. B, **2.** C, **3.** A, **4.** A, **5.** C, **6.** C

2. A Slice of Heaven
1. idyllic stone cottage, **2.** gentle river, **3.** clear blue sky, **4.** warm summer sun, **5.** typical English church, **6.** small green hill

3. Being a Business Person
1. E, **2.** D, **3.** F, **4.** A, **5.** C, **6.** B

4. Männer und Frauen beschreiben
1. pretty, **2.** gorgeous, **3.** handsome, **4.** good-looking, **5.** attractive

5. Some or any
1. any, **2.** anytime / anywhere, **3.** anywhere / anytime, **4.** somebody, **5.** something, **6.** anything, **7.** sometime

6. Right or wrong
1. wrong, **2.** wrong, **3.** right, **4.** right, **5.** right

7. Talking about Holiday
1. D, **2.** E, **3.** B, **4.** A, **5.** C

8. Beschreibungen – so wird's lebendiger
1. B, **2.** A, **3.** E, **4.** F, **5.** G, **6.** J, **7.** H, **8.** I, **9.** C, **10.** D, **11.** happy, **12.** quickly, **13.** quiet, **14.** beautiful, **15.** lovely, **16.** excellent, **17.** friendly, **18.** nice, **19.** annoyed, **20.** strange

9. Im Pub
1. D, **2.** F, **3.** E, **4.** A, **5.** C, **6.** B

10. Sich entschuldigen
1. sorry, **2.** I'm sorry, **3.** excuse me

11. How to place an order
Reihenfolge: **5.**, **2.**, **4.**, **3.**, **1.**

5 The Banshee

1. On the Bank of Strangford Lough
1. B, **2.** C, **3.** A, **4.** B, **5.** C, **6.** A

2. On the Road
1. B, **2.** F, **3.** A, **4.** E, **5.** C, **6.** D

3. Tageszeiten
1 a.m., morning (7 a.m.), 10 a.m., noon, afternoon (5 p.m.), evening (7 p.m.), night (11 p.m.), midnight (12 p.m.)

4. Die Uhr
1. eight o'clock (in the evening), **2.** half past eleven (in the morning), **3.** a quarter to four (in the morning), **4.** ten to eight (in the evening), **5.** a quarter past nine (in the evening), **6.** five minutes past four (in the morning)

5. Das Datum
USA: 5 / 1 / 17, 8 / 26 / 18, 3 / 5 / 20
GB: 1 May 17 (1 / 5 / 17), 26 August 18 (26 / 8 / 18), 5 March 20 (5 / 3 / 20)
11 / 8 / 2017: November 8, 2017 (8. November 2017)

6. Die Ordnungszahlen und das Datum
1. the fifth of January; **2.** the twenty-fourth of December; **3.** the fourteenth of February

7. Warum denn nicht Meter?
Lösung: (Distanz bis Whiterock:) a mile
1. B; **2.** C; **3.** A; **4.** D
5. 8,64 km, **6.** 162 cm, **7.** 6,3 m, **8.** 30,48 cm

8. Was ist passiert?
Richtige Reihenfolge: 5., 3., 2., 6., 4., 1.

9. Am Wasser
1 C; 2 A; 3 B; 4 E; 5 F; 6 D

10. Präpositionen
1. C; **2.** E; **3.** B; **4.** A; **5.** D

11. Gegensätze ziehen sich an
1. C; **2.** A; **3.** B; **4.** E; **5.** D

12. Ort vor Zeit
1. Dylan was near Whiterock shortly before midnight. / Shortly before midnight, Dylan was near Whiterock.
2. He wanted to hide on Sketrick Island that day until midnight. / That day, he wanted to hide on Sketrick Island until midnight.
3. Women ask men to marry them in Ireland every year on that very day. / In Ireland, women ask men to marry them every year on that very day.

6 The Next Step

1. A Perfect Day
1. A und B; **2.** C, **3.** B und C; **4.** A und C; **5.** B; **6.** C

2. Eigenschaften
1. happy, **2.** fine, **3.** talkative, **4.** cheerful, **5.** unhappy, **6.** not fine, **7.** silent, **8.** nervous
Gerald is (A) not fine. He is (B) silent and (C) nervous.

3. The Weather
1. E, **2.** F, **3.** B, **4.** C, **5.** D, **6.** A

4. The Landscape
1. D, **2.** E, **3.** B, **4.** A, **5.** C, **6.** F

5. In the Middle of the River
1. wrong, **2.** right, **3.** wrong, **4.** right, **5.** wrong

6. Go, go, go
1. Have a go!, **2.** Let's go!, **3.** You go first.
4. have a go, **5.** let's go, **6.** went first.

7. Kleine Wörter
1. D, **2.** A, **3.** B, **4.** C
5. Actually, **6.** However, **7.** Instead,
8. for a moment

8. Going To-Future
1. Gerald is going to pour Emma another large glass of champagne.
2. Gerald is going to say nothing for a few seconds.
3. Gerald is going to check that the small box is still in his shorts pocket.

9. The Proposal
Richtige Reihenfolge: D, A, F, E, B, C

10. Immer in Bewegung
1. H; **2.** C; **3.** F; **4.** G; **5.** K; **6.** E; **7.** J; **8.** A; **9.** B; **10.** I; **11.** D

11. Das Adverb
1. -ly, **2.** heavily, **3.** quietly, **4.** clumsily

12. Verliebt - verlobt - verheiratet
to propose to somebody
1. B, **2.** E / A, **3.** F, **4.** G, **5.** D / C

7 It Could be Worse

1. A Trip to Lake Windermere
1. B, **2.** C, **3.** C, **4.** B, **5.** C, **6.** C

2. Let's Go Camping
1. E, **2.** A, **3.** B, **4.** F, **5.** C, **6.** D

3. In a Thunderstorm
1. floods, **2.** clouds, **3.** rain, **4.** winds, **5.** lightning

4. Will-Future
1. will (not), **2.** Verb in der Grundform bzw. Infinitiv, **3.** She will open the wine, **4.** A little rain will not / won't be a problem for us.

5. Opposites
1. D, **2.** E, **3.** A, **4.** C, **5.** B
6. warm <> cold, **7.** romantic <> unromantic, **8.** dry <> wet, **9.** huge <> tiny, **10.** happy <> unhappy

6. What is correct?
1. B, **2.** A, **3.** B, **4.** A, **5.** B, **6.** A

7. Unregelmäßige Adjektive steigern
1. worse, **2.** worst, **3.** better

8. Adverbien steigern
1. badly, **2.** less, **3.** best

9. Adjektiv oder Adverb?
1. quickly, **2.** carefully, **3.** athletic, **4.** terribly, **5.** hard, **6.** heavily, **7.** slowly, **8.** clever, **9.** less

10. Das Partizip Präsens
1. covering, **2.** squeaking, **3.** sinking, **4.** moving, **5.** Lifting his leg, he began to climb onto the roof. **6.** Screaming, Liz dropped the bottle of wine she was holding.

11. If-Satz Typ I + II (Bedingungssätze)
1. It was beautiful, Duncan thought, and if he could repair the roof quickly, he was sure that Liz would enjoy the holiday. **2.** I think I can fix it, if I move this.

12. Would you...?
1. B (Bedingungssatz), **2.** D (höflicher Vorschlag), **3.** A (höfliche Frage), **4.** C (höfliche Bitte)

13. Typ I oder Typ II?
1. collapsed, **2.** could go, **3.** cannot fix, **4.** will take

14. When or if?
1. nicht sicher, **2.** sicher
3. If, **4.** When, **5.** if

15. What a Mess!
1. E, **2.** D, **3.** A, **4.** B, **5.** F, **6.** C

16. It Could be Worse
1. never mind / it doesn't matter, **2.** don't worry / it doesn't matter, **3.** don't worry, **4.** it could be worse / it doesn't matter, **5.** no problem

8 Don't Panic

1. A Trip in a Snow Storm
1. B, **2.** A, **3.** B, **4.** A, **5.** C, **6.** A

2. In the Car
1. B, **2.** A, **3.** F, **4.** E, **5.** D, **6.** C

3. Es ist Winter
1. C, **2.** B, **3.** A, **4.** D, **5.** E

4. On the Phone
1. E, **2.** C, **3.** D, **4.** B, **5.** A

5. Was gehört alles zu Weihnachten?
1. snow, **2.** presents, **3.** mistletoe, **4.** christmas cards, **5.** christmas tree

6. Mixed Bag
1. I'm going to be, **2.** am, **3.** is, **4.** fell, **5.** met, **6.** will be

7. Right or Wrong?
1. right, **2.** wrong, **3.** right, **4.** wrong, **5.** wrong

8. Ordnungszahlen
1. first, **2.** second, 3 third, **4.** -th, **5.** third, **6.** first, **7.** eighth

9. To have a Baby
1. large, pregnant stomach, **2.** my waters have broken, **3.** hospital, **4.** midwife, **5.** to have a baby

10. The Baby has arrived
1. C, **2.** D, **3.** B, **4.** F, **5.** E, **6.** A

11. Müssen und Sollen
1. must, **2.** need to, **3.** have to

12. Can vs. May
1. can, **2.** may, **3.** can, **4.** can, **5.** may

13. Reported Speech
1. Matthew says that his mother is not going to be happy.
2. Matthew says that she hates it when people are late.
3. Matthew says that she normally serves Christmas lunch at two.

14. Imperative
1. Grundform, **2.** don't / do not, **3.** Come in, please. **4.** Don't tell Mom I forgot the way home.

15. Das Present Perfect
My waters have broken.
1. have, **2.** has, **3.** -ed, **4.** dritte bzw. unregelmäßige;
5. hasn't said, **6.** have begun,
7. have just remembered, **8.** have known

16. Present Perfect oder Simple Past?
1. met, **2.** didn't know, **3.** have you ever seen, **4.** have just thought, **5.** didn't believe, **6.** became, **7.** have changed

17. When the Kids Get Older
1. E, **2.** A, **3.** C, **4.** B, **5.** F, **6.** D

18. Word Master
1. remember, **2.** quietly, **3.** waters, **4.** my, **5.** need, **6.** hospital, **7.** mother's, **8.** midwife, **9.** what, **10.** know, **11.** where, **12.** house, **13.** about, **14.** his, **15.** steering, **16.** when, **17.** the, **18.** snow, **19.** see, **20.** light

19. Grammar Master
1. were, **2.** hard, **3.** couldn't, **4.** signal of their mobile, **5.** broke, **6.** mountain bikers, **7.** knew

9 The Wrong Bag

1. Out in the Street
1. A, **2.** C, **3.** A, **4.** B, **5.** B, **6.** C

2. A Touristy Look...
1. C, **2.** D, **3.** F, **4.** B, **5.** A, **6.** E

3. TV, TV, TV
A. adverts, B. television screen, C. movies, D. the news, **5.** remote control

4. A Pretty Ugly Street
1. what does Jake see: adverts on TV screens, colours, giant faces, clips from movies, news headlines, commercials
2. what does Jake smell: food (the scent of hotdogs, onions, tomatoes, fries or donuts), cigarettes, alcohol, garbage and vomit, sweat
3. what does Jake hear: the horns of the big yellow taxis, music from the bars and restaurants, voices in different languages

5. Streetwear
casual clothes: t-shirt, jeans, hoodie, skirt
business clothes: shirt, blouse, suit, blazer, skirt

6. The Bag
1. A, **2.** C, **3.** B, **4.** B, **5.** A, **6.** A

7. The People of New York
1. D, **2.** E, **3.** B, **4.** F, **5.** A, **6.** C

8. Kleine Wörter
1. but, **2.** where, **3.** simply, **4.** again, then, **5.** then, but

9. Wortstellung

1. Yesterday, Jake was very nervous. / Jake was very nervous yesterday.
2. He slowly moved towards the crowd.
3. Back then, he needed to think. / He needed to think back then.
4. He wanted to take the bag carefully / He carefully wanted to take the bag. / Carefully, he wanted to take the bag.
5. When he had stolen the bag, he often looked around.

10. The Wrong Bag

1. A und B, **2.** A, **3.** C, **4.** B, **5.** C, **6.** B

11. Let's Put the Whole Story Together

1. wrong, **2.** wrong, **3.** right, **4.** wrong, **5.** right

12. Who vs. Which

1. who, **2.** which, **3.** which, **4.** who, **5.** who

13. Relativsätze mit / ohne Komma

1. (kein Komma), **2.** The NYPD, which is the police in New York, are chasing a man. **3.** Jake, who has no idea what is inside the bag, runs away. **4.** The bag, which he has stolen, is the wrong bag. **5.** (kein Komma), **6.** Now Jake, who is actually a thief, is a hero.

14. Relativsätze

1. Jake, who is a young boy, is a hero.
2. He stole a bag in which was a bomb.
3. He ran away from the man who wanted his bag back.
4. The police pushed the man, who was a terrorist, to the ground.

15. Word Master

1. sure, **2.** really, **3.** different, **4.** has, **5.** map, **6.** use, **7.** only, **8.** does, **9.** watch, **10.** by, **11.** looks, **12.** made, **13.** leather, **14.** that, **15.** quick, **16.** never, **17.** bag.

16. Grammar Master

1. slowly, **2.** grabbed, **3.** ran, **4.** when, **5.** was, **6.** some, **7.** has, **8.** must, **9.** leave, **10.** run

17. NYPD

1. C, **2.** B, **3.** D, **4.** E, **5.** F, **6.** A
Reihenfolge: 6, 1, 3, 2, 4, 5

10 Case Closed

1. A Hot Day in Court

1. A, **2.** C, **3.** B, **4.** C, **5.** B, **6.** B

2. In the Courtroom

1. B, **2.** G, **3.** F, **4.** H, **5.** C, **6.** A, **7.** E, **8.** D
H 1., F 2., B 3., A 4., D 5., C 6., E 7., G 8.

3. The Judge

1. B, **2.** C, **3.** A, **4.** D

4. Die Wiederholungszahlen

1. once, **2.** several times, **3.** twice, **4.** five times
5. Once bitten, twice shy. = Gebranntes Kind scheut das Feuer.

5. Once vs. Ones

1. Once, **2.** ones, **3.** once

6. One vs. Ones

1. Subjekt, **2.** one, **3.** ones
4. one, **5.** one, **6.** ones

7. Verben mit -ing

1. Nick dislikes having to sit in a hot room.
2. He doesn't like working overtime today.

8. How the Story Unfolds...

1. F, **2.** C, **3.** A, **4.** G, **5.** D, **6.** E, **7.** B

9. Right or Wrong?

1. right, **2.** right, **3.** wrong, **4.** right, **5.** wrong

10. Murder they say...
1. C, **2.** A, **3.** B

11. -ing-Formen
1. Manchmal kann der Beruf des Gerichtsprotokollanten langweilig sein.
2. Aber dann und wann hört Nick faszinierende Dinge im Gericht.
3. Er erzählt gern Geschichten in der Kneipe.
4. Sie warten gerade darauf, dass die Jury zu einer Entscheidung gelangt.
5. Er stößt eine Feuerschutztür zu seinem persönlichen Raucherbereich auf.
6. Das Gefühl der Sonne auf seinem Gesicht ist gut.
7. Heute Abend ist ein guter Abend, um etwas trinken zu gehen, denkt er, und er entscheidet gerade, wen er anrufen wird, als er eine Frauenstimme hört.
8. Er riskiert ein paar Schritte in Richtung der Stimme.
9. Die Frau sieht, dass er sie anschaut.
10. Er geht die Stufen hinauf zurück und fühlt sich verwirrt und unsicher.

12. Wie war das nochmal mit den Zeiten?
1. jetzt gerade (in diesem Augenblick), **2.** gerade, **3.** als, **4.** Feststellung

13. Gegenteile
1. F, **2.** H, **3.** G, **4.** C, **5.** E, **6.** A, **7.** D, **8.** B

14. In the News
1. woman, **2.** premeditated murder, **3.** stabbed, **4.** jury, **5.** make a verdict, **6.** mobile phone, **7.** who, **8.** court room, **9.** evidence, **10.** recording device, **11.** recorded, **12.** charged with murder

15. Die Zeiten
1. is sitting, **2.** has just entered, **3.** looks, **4.** have come, **5.** killed, **6.** tried, **7.** being, **8.** sentence, **9.** is talking, **10.** is looking, **11.** doesn't blink, **12.** thinks, **13.** is

16. Word Master
1. that, **2.** something, **3.** doesn't like, **4.** savage, **5.** violence, **6.** knows, **7.** only, **8.** feels, **9.** judge, **10.** nothing, **11.** looks, **12.** device, **13.** light

17. Grammar Master
1. If, **2.** sees, **3.** is blinking, **4.** really, **5.** now, **6.** once, **7.** angrily

11 The Best Place

1. A New Place
1. B, **2.** B, **3.** A, **4.** B, **5.** C, **6.** B

2. The House
1. E, **2.** F, **3.** A, **4.** C, **5.** B, **6.** D

3. The DIY-Couple
1. D, **2.** F, **3.** E, **4.** A, **5.** C, **6.** B

4. Proverbs
1. Buying the pig in a poke.
2. D, **3.** E, **4.** B, **5.** C, **6.** A
7. Viele Hände machen (der Arbeit) bald ein Ende.

5. Das Past Perfect
1. had passed, **2.** had moved, **3.** had, **4.** Grundform, **5.** -ed, **6.** unregelmäßige Verbform, **7.** had moved, **8.** started, **9.** discovered, **10.** had found, **11.** had had to, **12.** could

6. A Treasure in a Small Box
1. C, **2.** C, **3.** B, **4.** B, **5.** A, **6.** B

7. The Rooms of a House

1. D, **2.** A, **3.** F, **4.** E, **5.** B, **6.** C, **7.** larder, **8.** dining room, **9.** entrance room

8. I tell you...

1. summon, **2.** inquire, **3.** ask, **4.** answer, **5.** mutter

6. inquire, ask, **7.** reply, answer, **8.** mutter, **9.** ask, inquire, **10.** answer, reply

9. In the Retirement Home

1. E, **2.** F, **3.** B, **4.** A, **5.** C, **6.** D

10. Getting Sick

1. B, **2.** D, **3.** E, **4.** A, **5.** C

11. The Passive Voice

1. was pushed, **2.** was introduced,

3. to be (hier im Beispiel: was / were = Simple Past), **4.** Grundform, -ed,

5. unregelmäßige Verbform.

6. The house was renovated by Edward and Lynn. **7.** They are told to wait in the hallway by the doctor. **8.** Mrs Sinclair is pushed into the hallway by a nurse.

9. Mr Taylor gave them the address.

10. The nurse introduced the woman as Beth.

11. Beth hid the photos in the wall.

12. If vs. when vs. unless vs. whether

1. whether, **2.** if, **3.** When, **4.** If, **5.** unless

A

	a.m.	*Vormittag*
	abbey	*Kloster*
	about	*über; wegen*
	above	*über, oberhalb*
to	**acquire**	*erwerben*
	actually	*tatsächlich, eigentlich*
	address	*Adresse*
	adult	*Erwachsene / r*
	advert, advertisement	*Werbeanzeige, Werbespot*
	advice	*Ratschlag*
to	**afford**	*sich leisten*
	afraid	*verängstigt, ängstlich*
	after	*nach(dem)*
	afternoon	*Nachmittag*
	again	*wieder*
	against	*gegen*
	age	*Alter*
	ago	*vor,früher*
	air	*Luft*
	all	*alle*
	all day	*den ganzen Tag*
	All rise	*Erheben Sie sich*
	all the way	*den ganzen Weg*
	almost	*fast*
	alone	*allein*
	along	*entlang*
	already	*schon*
	although	*obwohl*
	always	*immer*
	and	*und*
	angry	*böse, ärgerlich*
	annoyed	*genervt, verärgert*
	another	*ein andere / r / s*
to	**answer**	*antworten*
	anything	*irgendetwas*
	apart from	*abgesehen von, außer*
to	**appear**	*auftauchen, erscheinen*
	area	*Gebiet, Gegend*
to	**argue**	*argumentieren, streiten*
	arm	*Arm*
	around	*herum*
to	**arrive**	*ankommen*
	as … as	*so … wie*
to	**ask**	*fragen*
to	**ask for**	*fragen nach, bitten um*
	at	*an, bei*
	at night	*nachts*
	attic	*Speicher, Dachboden*
	attractive	*attraktiv*
	avalanche	*Lawine*
	awake	*wach*
	away	*weg*

B

	baby bottle	*Babyfläschchen*
	Babygro®	*Strampler*
	back	*zurück*
	back stairs	*Hintertreppe*
	back up	*zurück nach oben*
	backpack	*Rucksack*
	backstreet	*Seitensträßchen*
	bag	*Tasche*
	balance	*Gleichgewicht*
	bank	*Ufer*
	banshee	*Todesfee*
	bar	*Gitterstab, Bar*
	barred window	*vergittertes Fenster*
	bartender	*Barkeeper*
to	**bathe**	*baden*
	bathroom	*Badezimmer*
to	**be about to do sth.**	*gerade etw. tun wollen*
to	**be arrested**	*verhaftet werden*
to	**be back**	*zurück sein*
to	**be called**	*heißen*
	Be careful!	*Sei / Seien Sie vorsichtig!*
to	**be covered**	*bedeckt sein*
to	**be determined**	*entschlossen sein*
to	**be divorced**	*geschieden sein*
to	**be engaged**	*verlobt sein*
to	**be joking**	*einen Scherz machen*
to	**be late**	*sich verspäten*
to	**be lost**	*sich verirrt haben*

to	**be scared**	*Angst haben*
to	**be sure**	*sicher sein*
to	**be tired of doing sth.**	*keine Lust mehr haben, etw. zu tun*
	beautiful	*(wunder)schön*
	because	*weil*
	because of	*wegen*
to	**become**	*werden; annehmen*
	bedroom	*Schlafzimmer*
	beer	*Bier*
	before	*vor(her)*
to	**begin**	*anfangen*
	behind	*hinter*
	belly	*Magen, Bauch*
to	**belong to**	*gehören*
	belongings (pl.)	*Besitztümer, Habseligkeiten*
	beloved	*geliebt*
	below	*darunter*
	beside	*neben*
	best	*beste/r/s*
	better	*besser/e/r/s*
	between	*zwischen*
	bicycle	*Fahrrad*
	big	*groß*
	bin	*(AE) Mülleimer*
	a bit	*ein bisschen*
	bit	*Stückchen*
	black	*schwarz*
	black ice	*Glatteis*
	blazer	*Blazer, Jackett*
to	**bleed from**	*bluten aus*
	blonde	*blond*
	blouse	*Bluse*
to	**blow away sth.**	*etwas wegpusten*
	blue	*blau*
to	**blush**	*erröten*
	boat	*Boot*
	book	*Buch*
	both	*beide*
	bottle	*Flasche*
	bottom	*Boden, Grund*
	box	*Schachtel*
	boy	*Junge*
	boyfriend	*Freund*
	brace	*Zahnspange*
	brave	*tapfer, mutig*
to	**break**	*(zer)brechen, kaputtgehen*
to	**breathe**	*atmen*
	breeze	*Brise*
	bridge	*Brücke*
	brief	*kurz*
	bright	*hell, strahlend*
	brochure	*Prospekt*
	broken	*kaputt; geplatzt*
	broomstick	*Besenstiel*
	brother	*Bruder*
	brown	*braun*
	budget	*Budget*
	business	*Geschäft, Betrieb*
	business people	*Geschäftsleute*
	busy	*beschäftigt*
	but	*aber*
to	**buy**	*kaufen*
to	**buy the pig in a poke**	*die Katze im Sack kaufen*
	by	*neben; bis*
	by now	*inzwischen*

C

	calmly	*ruhig, gelassen*
	camera	*Kamera*
	camp bed	*Camping-Bett*
	camping cooker	*Camping-Kocher*
	can	*können*
	captain	*Kapitän*
to	**capture a moment**	*den Moment festhalten*
	car	*Auto*
	caravan	*Wohnwagen*
to	**care about sb./sth.**	*sich um jdn./etw. kümmern, sich sorgen*
	careful	*vorsichtig*
to	**carry**	*tragen*
	case	*Fall*
	castle	*Burg*

	casual	*locker; Freizeit-*
	causeway	*Damm, erhöhter Fußweg*
	cellar	*Keller*
	centre	*Mitte*
	certainly	*sicherlich*
	champagne	*Champagner*
to	**change**	*sich verändern*
to	**chase**	*jagen*
to	**check**	*überprüfen*
	cheerful	*fröhlich*
	chef	*Chefkoch*
	child (pl. children)	*Kind*
	children's room	*Kinderzimmer*
	China	*China; Porzellan*
	Chinese	*Chinese, Chinesin; chinesisch*
	chocolate	*Schokolade*
	christmas card	*Weihnachtskarte*
	christmas tree	*Weihnachtsbaum*
	church	*Kirche*
	clear	*klar*
	clearly	*klar*
	clever	*schlau, klug*
to	**climb up**	*hinaufklettern*
	clip	*Spot*
	clock	*Uhr*
to	**close**	*schließen*
	close	*nahe*
	clothes (pl.)	*Kleidung*
	cloud	*Wolke*
	cloudy	*wolkig*
	coach	*Reisebus*
	coast	*Küste*
	coat	*Mantel*
	code of law	*Gesetzbuch*
	cold	*kalt*
	colour	*Farbe*
to	**come**	*kommen*
to	**come from**	*hier: ertönen; kommen von/aus*
	comfortable	*bequem*
	commercial	*Werbung, Werbespot*

	compartment	*Zugabteil*
to	**complete**	*vervollständigen*
	completely	*völlig, total*
to	**concentrate**	*sich konzentrieren*
	concrete	*Beton*
	concrete bed	*Betonbett*
	conductor	*Schaffner*
	confused	*verwirrt*
to	**consider**	*erwägen*
to	**consist of**	*bestehen aus*
	constantly	*ständig*
to	**continue**	*weitermachen*
	contract	*Vertrag*
	cool	*kühl*
	cot	*Babybett*
	counter	*Theke*
	country	*Land*
	countryside	*Landschaft*
	couple	*Paar, Pärchen*
	court clerk	*Gerichtsdiener*
	court hammer	*Gerichtshammer*
	court reporter	*Gerichtsreporter*
	courthouse	*Gericht*
	courtroom	*Gerichtssaal*
to	**cover**	*bedecken*
	cover	*Schicht, Decke*
	cow	*Kuh*
	crack	*Riss*
	crash	*Schlag, Zusammenstoß*
	crazy	*verrückt*
	creature	*Wesen*
	crime	*Verbrechen*
to	**cross**	*überqueren*
	crossword	*Kreuzworträtsel*
	crowd	*Menschenmenge*
	crutch	*Krücke*
	cry	*Schrei*
to	**cry**	*rufen; weinen*
	cucumber	*Gurke*
	culture	*Kultur*
	cup	*Tasse*
	curiously	*neugierig*
	curtain	*Vorhang*

	Czech	*tschechisch; Tscheche, Tschechin*

D

	daft	*dumm, blöd*
	dangerous	*gefährlich*
to	**dare**	*sich trauen*
	dark	*dunkel*
	darkness	*Dunkelheit*
	darling	*Liebling*
	date	*Datum*
	day	*Tag*
	deceased	*verstorben*
	decent	*vernünftig*
to	**decide**	*entscheiden*
	deep	*tief*
	defence	*Strafverteidiger/in*
	defendant	*Angeklagte/r*
	delicious	*delikat, köstlich*
	dementia	*Demenz*
to	**describe**	*beschreiben*
	desert	*Wüste*
	desk	*Schreibtisch*
	despite	*trotz*
	detail	*Detail, Einzelheit*
	determined	*entschlossen*
	diaper	*Windel*
to	**die**	*sterben*
	difficult	*schwierig*
	dilapidated	*heruntergekommen*
	direction	*Richtung*
	directly	*direkt*
	dirt	*Dreck*
	dirty	*schmutzig*
	disappointed	*enttäuscht*
to	**discover**	*entdecken*
	discreet	*dezent*
	disease	*Krankheit*
	display	*Bildschirm*
	distance	*Entfernung*
	distant	*entfernt*
	distraction	*Ablenkung*
to	**disturb**	*stören*
	DIY-type	*Heimwerker-*
to	**do**	*tun*
	don't panic!	*Nur keine Panik!*
	don't worry	*das macht nichts*
	door	*Tür*
	doorstep	*Türschwelle*
	doorway	*Eingang*
	dot	*Tupfer, Punkt*
	down	*hinunter*
	dress	*Kleid*
	drill	*Bohrer*
to	**drink**	*trinken*
	drink	*Getränk*
	drip	*Tropfen*
	dripping	*tropf-, tropfend*
to	**drive**	*fahren (mit dem Auto)*
	dry	*trocken*
	due to	*infolge, wegen*
	dumb	*(AE) dumm*
	during	*während*
	dust	*Staub*
	Dutch	*holländisch; Holländer*

E

	each other	*einander*
	easily	*leicht*
	eastern	*östlich, Ost-*
to	**eat**	*essen*
	edge	*Rand*
	eighth	*der/die/das achte*
	elderly	*älter/e/r/s, Senioren-*
	elegant	*elegant*
to	**embrace**	*umarmen*
to	**emphasize**	*betonen*
	empty	*leer*
	engine	*Maschine, Motor*
	England	*England*
	English	*englisch; Engländer*
to	**enjoy**	*genießen*
	enough	*genug*
to	**enter**	*eintreten*
to	**enter court**	*den Gerichtssaal betreten*

	enthusiastic	*begeistert*
	enthusiastically	*enthusiastisch*
	entrance room	*Eingangsbereich*
	even	*sogar*
	even though	*obwohl*
	evening	*Abend*
	event	*Ereignis*
	every	*jede/r/s*
	everybody	*jede/r/s*
	evidence	*Beweis*
	exactly	*genau*
to	**exceed**	*übersteigen*
	excellent	*hervorragend*
	Excuse me!	*Entschuldigung!, Entschuldigen Sie bitte/ Entschuldige bitte, ...!*
to	**exit**	*hinausgehen*
	exotic	*exotisch*
to	**expect**	*erwarten*
	expensive	*teuer*
to	**experience**	*(mit)erleben*
to	**explain**	*erklären*
to	**explore**	*erkunden*
	expression	*Ausdruck*
	eye	*Auge*

F

	face	*Gesicht*
	fact	*Tatsache*
	fake	*erfunden, falsch*
to	**fall**	*fallen*
	familiar	*bekannt*
	family	*Familie*
	famous	*berühmt*
	fantastic	*fantastisch*
	far	*weit*
	fast	*schnell*
	fault	*Fehler*
	favourite	*Lieblings-*
	February	*Februar*
to	**feel**	*fühlen*
to	**feel defeated**	*sich besiegt fühlen*
to	**feel sick**	*sich schlecht fühlen, jdm. ist schlecht*
to	**feel sorry for sb.**	*Mitleid mit jdm. haben*
	female	*weiblich/e/r/s*
	a few	*ein paar*
	fifth	*der/die/das fünfte*
	figure	*Gestalt*
	final	*letzte/r/s, End-*
	finally	*schließlich*
to	**find**	*finden*
to	**find out**	*herausfinden*
	fine	*gut*
	finger	*Finger*
to	**finish**	*beenden*
	first	*zuerst; erste/r/s*
	fish and chips	*Fisch und Pommes Frites*
to	**fit**	*passen*
to	**fix**	*reparieren*
to	**flash**	*blinken*
	flask	*Thermosflasche*
	flat	*flach*
to	**flip through**	*durchblättern*
	flood	*Überflutung*
	floor	*Stockwerk; Boden*
	foggy	*neblig*
	folk music	*Folkmusik*
to	**follow**	*folgen*
	food	*Essen*
	fool	*Idiot*
	foot	*Fuß (auch Längenmaß, ca. 30 cm)*
	for	*für; seit*
	for a moment	*einen Augenblick lang*
	for ages	*seit Ewigkeiten*
	forehead	*Stirn*
	forest	*Wald*
to	**forget**	*vergessen*
	formal	*formell*
	former	*ehemalige/r/s*
	forward(s)	*vorwärts, nach vorn*
	four	*vier*
	fourth	*der/die/das vierte*
	France	*Frankreich*

	freckles (Pl.)	*Sommersprossen*
	French	*französisch; Franzose(n)*
	friend	*Freund/in*
	friendly	*freundlich*
	fries	*(AE) Pommes Frites*
	from	*von, aus*
	fruit	*Obst*
	full	*voll*
	funny	*lustig, seltsam*
	furious	*wütend*
	furniture	*Möbel*
	future	*Zukunft*

G

	garage	*Garage, Autowerkstatt*
	garbage	*(AE) Abfall*
	gear level	*Gangschaltung*
	gentle	*höflich, ruhig,*
	German	*deutsch; Deutsche/r*
	Germany	*Deutschland*
to	**get**	*erreichen, bekommen; werden*
to	**get a signal**	*Empfang haben*
to	**get divorced**	*sich scheiden lassen*
to	**get engaged**	*sich verloben*
to	**get hold of sth.**	*etwas zu fassen bekommen*
to	**get sb. back to**	*jdn. zurückbringen*
to	**get to know sb.**	*jdn. kennenlernen*
to	**get to sth.**	*etw. erreichen*
	ghost	*Geist*
	giant	*riesig*
	gift	*Geschenk*
	girl	*Mädchen*
	girlfriend	*Freundin*
to	**give sth. to so.**	*jdm. etw. geben*
	glass	*Glas*
	glasses (pl.)	*Brille*
	glaucoma	*Grüner Star*
to	**go on**	*weitermachen*
to	**go out**	*ausgehen*
	gold	*golden*
	good	*gut*
	good-looking	*gutaussehend*
	gorgeous	*wunderschön*
	gown	*Talar, Richterrobe; Kleid*
to	**grab**	*packen*
	grass	*Gras*
	great	*groß, großartig*
	green	*grün*
	grey	*grau*
	ground	*Erde, Boden*
	group	*Gruppe*
to	**guess**	*raten*
	guidebook	*Reiseführer (Buch)*
	guilty	*schuldig*
	guy	*Typ, Kerl*

H

	hair	*Haar(e)*
	half	*halb, Hälfte*
	hall	*Eingangshalle, Flur*
	hammer	*Hammer*
	hand	*Hand*
	handbreak	*Handbremse*
	handsome	*gutaussehend (Mann)*
to	**happen**	*geschehen*
	happy	*glücklich, froh*
	harbour	*Hafen*
to	**hate**	*hassen*
to	**have**	*haben*
to	**have a baby**	*ein Kind bekommen*
to	**have a go**	*etw. versuchen*
to	**have a look at sth.**	*etwas anschauen*
to	**have to**	*müssen*
	head	*Kopf*
to	**hear**	*hören*
	heart	*Herz*
	heart attack	*Herzinfarkt*
	heaven	*Himmel*
	heavy	*schwer*
	...the hell...	*zur Hölle*
to	**help**	*helfen*
to	**help out**	*aushelfen*
	helpful	*hilfsbereit*
	here	*hier*

	here we go	*los geht's*
	here you are	*bitte schön*
	hero	*Held*
to	**hesitate**	*zögern*
to	**hide**	*verstecken*
	high	*hoch*
to	**hike**	*wandern*
	hiking boots	*Wanderschuhe*
	hill	*Hügel*
to	**hit**	*treffen, hier: überfahren*
to	**hold out**	*hier: vorzeigen*
	hole	*Loch*
	holiday	*Urlaub*
	home	*Zuhause*
	honey	*(Kosewort:) Liebling*
	hoodie	*Kapuzenpullover*
	horn	*Hupe*
	horrible	*schrecklich*
	hospital	*Krankenhaus*
	hot	*heiß*
	hotel room	*Hotelzimmer*
	hour	*Stunde*
	house	*Haus*
	how	*wie*
	however	*aber, jedoch*
to	**hug**	*umarmen*
	huge	*groß, hier: breit*
	hundred	*Hundert*
	hungry	*hungrig*
to	**hurry up**	*sich beeilen*
to	**hurt**	*verletzen*
	husband	*Ehemann*

I

	I do love	*Ich mag das sehr*
	I'm sorry	*Entschuldigung!, Entschuldigen Sie bitte/Entschuldige bitte, ...!*
	icicle	*Eiszapfen*
	idea	*Idee, Ahnung*
	idyllic	*idyllisch*
	if	*wenn, falls*
to	**imagine**	*sich etw. vorstellen*
	immediately	*sofort*
	important	*wichtig*
	impossible	*unmöglich*
	impressive	*beeindruckend, eindrucksvoll*
	in	*in*
	in defence of	*zur Verteidigung von*
	in despair	*verzweifelt*
	in fact	*eigentlich*
	in front of	*vor (räumlich)*
	inch	*Zoll (2,54 cm)*
	incredibly	*unglaublich*
	indeed	*tatsächlich*
	indicator	*Blinker*
	infant	*Baby*
	injury	*Verletzung*
	innocent	*unschuldig*
to	**inquire**	*nachfragen*
	insane	*verrückt*
	inside	*innen (drin)*
	instead (of)	*stattdessen, anstatt (von)*
	intention	*Absicht*
to	**interest**	*interessieren*
	interesting	*interessant*
	into	*in (hinein)*
to	**introduce**	*vorstellen (jdm.); (neu) einführen*
to	**invite**	*einladen*
	Ireland	*Irland*
	Irish	*irisch; Ire/in*
	island	*Insel*
	it doesn't matter	*das macht nichts*
	it's fine	*es macht nichts, es ist in Ordnung*
	Italian	*italienisch; Italiener/in*
	Italy	*Italien*

J

	(a pair of) jeans	*Jeans*
	job	*Arbeit(sstelle)*
to	**join sb.**	*jmd. Gesellschaft leisten*

to	**join the gang**	*sich der Gang anschließen*
to	**joke**	*scherzen*
	journey	*Reise*
	judge	*Richter/in*
	judge's chamber	*Richterzimmer*
	judge's table	*Richtertisch*
to	**jump**	*springen*
to	**jump in**	*hineinspringen*
	just	*nur; gerade eben*

K

	keypad	*Tastatur*
	kid	*Kind*
to	**kill**	*töten*
	kind	*nett*
	kitchen	*Küche*
to	**kneel down**	*niederknien*
to	**knock**	*klopfen*
	knot	*Knoten*
to	**know**	*wissen, kennen*

L

to	**land**	*landen*
	language	*Sprache*
	large	*groß*
	last	*letzte/r/s*
	late	*spät*
to	**laugh**	*lachen*
	laughter	*Gelächter*
	lawyer	*Anwalt, Anwältin*
to	**lay parquet**	*Parkett verlegen*
to	**lead**	*hinführen*
	leap year	*Schaltjahr*
to	**learn**	*lernen*
to	**leave**	*verlassen*
	left	*links*
	leg	*Bein*
	less	*weniger*
to	**let sb. in**	*jdn. hereinlassen*
to	**lie**	*liegen*
	life	*Leben*
to	**lift**	*heben*
	light	*hell*
to	**light**	*beleuchten*
	lightning	*Blitz*
to	**like**	*mögen, gern haben*
	like	*wie*
	like the back of my hand	*wie meine Westentasche*
	line	*Linie*
	little	*klein, wenig*
	little more than	*wenig mehr als*
to	**live**	*leben, wohnen*
	living room	*Wohnzimmer*
	lobby	*Eingangsbereich, Lobby*
	local	*örtlich, aus der Gegend*
	location	*Platz, Ort*
	long	*lang*
to	**look at sb.**	*jdn. anschauen*
to	**look back**	*zurückschauen*
to	**look best**	*am besten aussehen*
to	**look for sth. / sb.**	*jdn. suchen*
to	**look fun**	*etw. sieht lustig aus*
to	**look over one's shoulder**	*über die/jds. Schulter schauen*
to	**lose sth. / sb.**	*etw/jdn. verlieren*
	loss	*Verlust*
	lost	*verloren*
	a lot	*viel*
	loud	*laut*
	lough	*See*
to	**love**	*lieben*
to	**love to do sth.**	*etwas sehr gerne tun*
	loveable	*liebenswert*
	lovely	*hübsch*
	low	*niedrig*
	luckily	*glücklicherweise*

M

to	**make a verdict**	*ein Urteil fällen*
to	**make oneself comfortable**	*es sich bequem machen*
to	**make s.o. chase s.b.**	*jdn. dazu veranlassen jdn. zu jagen*

to	**make s.o. feel tired**	*jmd. müde werden lassen*
to	**make sure**	*sich vergewissern*
	Maltese	*maltesisch; Malteser/in*
	man	*Mann*
to	**manage**	*etw einrichten können*
to	**manipulate**	*manipulieren*
	manslaughter	*Totschlag*
	many	*viele*
	mark	*Bluterguss, Mal*
	marriage	*Ehe*
to	**marry**	*heiraten*
to	**matter**	*ausmachen*
	maybe	*vielleicht*
to	**mean**	*meinen*
	meeting	*Konferenz; Treffen*
	memory	*Gedächtnis*
	mental	*verrückt*
	mess	*Durcheinander*
	middle	*Mitte, mitten (in)*
	midnight	*Mitternacht*
	midwife	*Hebamme*
	midwinter	*Mitte des Winters, Wintermitte*
	might	*könnte (vielleicht)*
	mile	*Meile (1,6 km)*
to	**mind**	*aufpassen auf, beachten; sich kümmern*
	minute	*Minute*
	mischievous	*boshaft, verschmitzt*
	mistletoe	*Mistelzweig*
to	**mix together**	*sich vermischen*
	mixture	*Mischung*
to	**moan**	*stöhnen*
	mobile phone	*Mobiltelefon, Handy*
	moment	*Moment*
	money	*Geld*
	month	*Monat*
	moon	*Mond*
	more	*mehr*
	morning	*Morgen*
	most	*meist/e/r/s*
	mother	*Mutter*
	mountain	*Berg*
	mountain biker	*Mountainbikefahrer/in*
	mouth	*Mund*
to	**move**	*(sich) bewegen; umziehen*
	movie	*(Kino-)Film*
	mud	*Schlamm*
	muddy	*schlammig*
	multiple	*viele*
	murder	*Mord*
to	**murmur**	*murmeln*
	music	*Musik*
	must	*müssen*
to	**mutter**	*murmeln*
	mutter	*Murmeln, Gemurmel*
	my God	*mein Gott*

N

	nail	*Nagel*
	narrow	*eng*
	near	*nahe, in der Nähe*
	nearly	*fast*
	neat	*hier: hübsch*
	neckerchief	*Halstuch*
	need	*müssen, brauchen*
	neighbour	*Nachbar/in*
	neighbourhood	*Nachbarschaft*
	nervous	*nervös*
	never	*niemals*
	never even	*noch überhaupt nicht*
	never mind	*macht nichts, ist doch egal*
	newborn	*Neugeborenes*
	newly	*neu*
	news	*Nachrichten*
	news headlines	*Schlagzeilen*
	newspaper	*Zeitung*
	next	*nächste/r/s*
	next to	*neben*
	nice	*nett*
	night	*Nacht*
	nightmare	*Alptraum*
	ninth	*der/die/das neunte*

	no more than	*nicht mehr als*
	no one	*niemand*
	no problem	*kein Problem*
	no worries	*Keine Sorge!*
to	**nod (one's head)**	*(mit dem Kopf) nicken*
	noise	*Lärm*
	noon	*Mittag*
	normal	*normal*
	north	*nördlich, nach Norden*
	North	*Norden*
	Northern Ireland	*Nordirland*
	nose	*Nase*
	not ... even	*nicht einmal*
	note	*Notiz*
	nothing	*nichts*
to	**notice**	*bemerken*
	now	*jetzt*
	nowhere	*nirgendwo*
	nurse	*Pfleger(in)*
	NYPD	*New Yorker Polizei*

O

	o'clock	*Uhr (Zeitangabe)*
	oar	*Ruder*
	obvious	*offensichtlich*
	occasion	*Gelegenheit*
	occasionally	*gelegentlich*
	of	*von*
	of course	*natürlich*
	offer	*Angebot*
	office	*Büro*
	old	*alt*
	on	*auf; an, am*
	once more	*noch einmal*
	one	*eine/r/s*
	onion	*Zwiebel*
	onlooker	*Betrachter, Zuschauer*
	only	*nur*
	onto	*auf...hinauf*
to	**open**	*öffnen*
	opinion	*Meinung*
	opposite	*gegenüber*
	or	*oder*
	ordinary	*gewöhnlich*
to	**organise**	*organisieren*
	other	*andere/r/s*
	out	*hinaus*
	out here/there	*hier/dort draußen*
	outside	*außen, draußen*
	oven	*Ofen*
	own	*eigene/r/s*
	owner	*Eigentümer/in*

P

	p.m.	*Nachmittag; Abend*
	pacifier	*Schnuller*
to	**pack**	*packen*
	pack	*Packung*
	a pair of	*ein Paar*
	pale	*blass, fahl*
to	**panic**	*in Panik geraten*
	parents (Pl.)	*Eltern*
	part	*Teil*
to	**pass**	*(hinüber)reichen*
	passenger seat	*Beifahrersitz*
	past	*nach (zeitlich); vorbei an*
to	**pat**	*streicheln*
	path	*Pfad*
	peace and quiet	*Ruhe und Frieden*
	people	*Leute, Menschen*
	peoples (Pl.)	*Völker*
	perfect	*perfekt*
	perfume	*Parfüm*
to	**phone sb.**	*jdn. anrufen*
	picnic blanket	*Picknickdecke*
	picture	*Bild*
	picturesque	*malerisch*
	piece	*Stück*
	place	*Platz*
to	**plaster**	*pflastern*
	plastic	*Plastik*
	play	*Abspielen*
	Please be seated!	*Bitte nehmen Sie Platz!*
	pliers (Pl.)	*Zange*

	pocket	*Tasche (in Kleidungsstück)*
	pocketlamp	*Taschenlampe*
to	**point to**	*zeigen auf*
to	**point up**	*hinaufzeigen*
	pointed roof	*Spitzdach*
	poison	*Gift*
to	**poke into**	*in etwas herumstochern*
	Polish	*polnisch; Pole/n, Polin*
	polite	*höflich*
	Portuguese	*Portugiese, Portugiesin; portugiesisch*
	positive	*positiv*
	possible	*möglich*
	possibly	*vermutlich*
	post	*Pfosten*
to	**pour**	*einschenken*
to	**pour down**	*in Strömen regnen*
	pram	*Kinderwagen*
to	**pregnant**	*schwanger*
	premeditated murder	*vorsätzlicher Mord*
	prepared	*bereit, vorbereitet*
	present	*Geschenk*
to	**press**	*drücken*
to	**pretend**	*vorgeben*
	pretty	*hübsch*
	prison	*Gefängnis*
	probably	*wahrscheinlich*
	problem	*Problem*
	profession	*Beruf*
to	**promise**	*versprechen*
	promotion	*Beförderung*
	proof	*Beweis*
to	**propose to s.b.**	*jemandem einen Heiratsantrag machen*
	prosecution	*Staatsanwaltschaft*
	prospect	*Aussicht*
	provider	*Anbieter*
	pub	*Kneipe*
to	**pull**	*ziehen*
to	**pull one's hand away**	*seine Hand wegziehen*
to	**pull s.o. up**	*jdn. hochziehen*
	purple	*violett*
to	**push sth. open**	*aufdrücken*
to	**put**	*setzen, stellen, legen*
to	**put together**	*zusammensetzen*

Q

	question	*Frage*
	quick	*schnell*
	quiet	*ruhig, still*
	quite	*ziemlich*

R

	rain	*Regen*
	rainy	*regnerisch*
to	**reach**	*erreichen*
to	**read**	*lesen*
	ready	*bereit*
	real	*echt*
to	**realise**	*bemerken*
	reality	*Wirklichkeit*
	recently	*kürzlich*
to	**record**	*aufnehmen*
	recording device	*Aufnahmegerät*
to	**recover**	*sich erholen*
to	**recover from one's shock**	*sich von seinem Schock erholen*
	red	*rot*
	reflection	*Reflektion, Spiegelung*
to	**regain**	*wiedererlangen*
to	**relax**	*entspannen*
to	**remember**	*sich erinnern an*
to	**remodel**	*renovieren*
	remote control	*Fernbedienung*
to	**repeat**	*wiederholen*
to	**reply**	*antworten*
	reputation	*Ruf*
to	**rest**	*sich ausruhen*
	retirement home	*Altersheim*
to	**return**	*zurückkehren*
to	**reveal**	*enthüllen*
	rhythm	*Rhythmus*
	riddle	*Rätsel*

	right behind sb.	*direkt hinter jdm.*
to	**ring**	*klingeln*
	river	*Fluss*
	road	*Straße*
	road sign	*Straßenschild*
	romantic	*romantisch*
	roof	*Dach*
	room	*Raum*
	rowing boat	*Ruderboot*
	ruins	*Ruinen*
	rule	*Regel*
to	**rumble**	*knurren*
to	**run**	*rennen*
to	**run away**	*wegrennen*
	rush job	*hektische Angelegenheit*
	Russian	*russisch; Russe/n, Russin*
	rusty	*eingerostet*

S

	sad	*traurig*
	sadness	*Traurigkeit*
to	**sail up**	*entgegen-/herbeisegeln*
	same	*gleich/e/r/s*
	sandwich	*Sandwich, belegtes Brot*
	sane	*bei Verstand, normal, zurechnungsfähig*
	savage	*wild*
	saw	*Säge*
to	**say**	*sagen*
to	**scare s.o.**	*jdn. erschrecken*
to	**scatter**	*verstreuen*
	scent	*Duft, Geruch*
	scissors (pl.)	*Schere*
	Scottish	*schottisch; Schotte/n, Schottin*
	scout	*Pfadfinder*
	scream	*Schrei, Aufschrei*
to	**scream**	*schreien*
	screen	*Bildschirm*
	screw	*Schraube*
	sea	*Meer*
to	**search**	*(ab)suchen*
	seaside	*am Meer/See (gelegen)*
	seaside town	*Küstenstädtchen*
	seat	*Sitz, Platz*
	seatbelt	*Gurt*
	second	*Sekunde; zweiter*
to	**see**	*sehen*
to	**seem to do sth.**	*scheinbar etw. tun*
to	**seem very strange**	*äußerst seltsam erscheinen*
	selection	*Auswahl*
to	**sell**	*verkaufen*
	sentence	*Satz*
	serious	*ernst*
to	**serve**	*servieren, bedienen*
to	**serve lunch**	*das Mittagessen servieren*
	seventh	*der/die/das siebte*
	several	*mehrere, einige*
to	**shake (one's head)**	*(den Kopf) schütteln*
	shall we	*sollen wir*
	shirt	*Hemd*
to	**shiver**	*schaudern*
	shop	*Laden*
	shore	*Ufer*
	short	*kurz*
	shorts pocket	*Hosentasche*
	should	*sollte*
	shoulder	*Schulter*
	shoulder bag	*Schultertasche*
	shout	*lauter Ruf*
to	**shout**	*rufen*
to	**show**	*zeigen*
	shower	*Dusche*
to	**shriek**	*kreischen*
to	**shriek in surprise**	*vor Überraschung aufschreien*
	side	*Seite*
to	**sigh**	*seufzen*
	sign	*Schild*
to	**sign**	*unterschreiben*
	sign of life	*Lebenszeichen*
	signal	*Signal*

	silent	*ruhig, still*
	silhouette	*Silhouette*
	simply	*einfach*
	since	*seit (Zeitpunkt)*
to	**sink**	*sinken*
	sink	*Waschbecken*
	sister	*Schwester*
to	**sit down**	*sich hinsetzen*
to	**sit on**	*sitzen auf*
	situation	*Situation*
	six	*sechs*
	sixth	*der/die/das sechste*
	skin	*Haut*
	skirt	*Rock*
	sky	*Himmel*
	skyscraper	*Wolkenkratzer*
to	**sleep**	*schlafen*
	sleeping bag	*Schlafsack*
	slice	*Stück, Scheibe*
to	**slip**	*ausrutschen*
	slow	*langsam*
to	**slow**	*langsamer werden*
	small	*klein*
	smart	*hier: schick*
	smell	*Geruch*
	smile	*Lächeln*
to	**smile**	*lächeln*
	snap	*Schnappschuss*
	sneakers	*(AE) Turnschuhe*
to	**sniff**	*schnüffeln*
to	**snow**	*schneien*
	snow	*Schnee*
	snowflake	*Schneeflocke*
	snowplough	*Schneepflug*
	so	*also*
	soft	*weich*
to	**solve**	*lösen*
	some	*einige, etwas*
	someone	*jemand*
	something	*etwas*
	sometimes	*manchmal*
	son	*Sohn*
	soon	*bald*
	sorry	*Entschuldigung*
	sort of	*Art von*
	sound	*Geräusch, Klang*
to	**speak**	*sprechen*
	special	*besondere/r/s*
	speech	*Rede*
	splash	*Platschen*
	spooky	*unheimlich, gruselig*
	sports car	*Sportwagen*
	squeaking	*quietschend*
to	**squeal**	*kreischen, quietschen*
to	**stab**	*erstechen*
	stack	*Stapel*
to	**stand**	*stehen*
to	**stand up**	*aufstehen*
	star	*Stern*
to	**start**	*anfangen*
	state of mind	*Geisteszustand*
to	**stay**	*bleiben*
to	**stay away from sth./sb.**	*sich von etw./jdm. fernhalten*
to	**steal**	*stehlen*
	steam train	*Dampflok*
	steering wheel	*Lenkrad*
to	**step**	*treten*
	step	*Schritt, Stufe*
	stepping stones	*Trittsteine*
	still	*immer noch*
	stomach	*Bauch; Magen*
	stone	*Stein*
	stone path	*Steinpfad*
	stone wall	*Steinmauer*
to	**stop**	*anhalten, aufhören*
	storage room	*Speisekammer, Lagerraum*
	storm	*Sturm*
	story	*Geschichte*
	straight	*gerade*
	strange	*seltsam*
	stranger	*Fremde/r*
	stroke	*Schlaganfall*
	stronger	*stärker/e/r/s*
to	**struggle**	*sich abmühen*

	stupid	*dumm*
	suddenly	*plötzlich*
to	**suffer a stroke**	*einen Schlaganfall erleiden*
	suit	*Anzug*
to	**suit someone best**	*etw. passt jdm. am Besten*
	suitcase	*Koffer*
	summary	*Zusammenfassung*
	summer	*Sommer*
to	**summon**	*herbeirufen*
	sun	*Sonne*
	Sunday	*Sonntag*
	sunglasses (Pl.)	*Sonnenbrille*
	sunny	*sonnig*
	supper	*Abendessen*
to	**suppose**	*annehmen*
	surprise	*Überraschung*
	sweat	*Schweiß*
	sweaty	*verschwitzt*
to	**swim**	*schwimmen*
	Swiss	*schweizerisch; Schweizer / in*

T

	T-shirt	*T-Shirt*
	table	*Tisch*
	tablet	*Tablet(computer)*
to	**take**	*nehmen*
to	**take a picture**	*ein Bild machen*
to	**take over**	*übernehmen*
to	**talk**	*sprechen, sich unterhalten*
	talkative	*gesprächig*
	tall	*groß*
	tame	*zahm*
	tea	*Tee*
	tear	*Träne*
	teenager	*Teenager*
	teeth (Pl.)	*Zähne*
	television screen	*Fernsehbildschirm*
to	**tell**	*erzählen*
	ten	*zehn*
	tent	*Zelt*
	tenth	*der / die / das zehnte*
	terrace	*Terrasse*
	terrible	*schrecklich*
	terrified	*verängstigt*
	terrifying	*furchteinflößend*
to	**testify**	*aussagen*
	than	*als*
	that	*das*
	the other day	*letztens*
	then	*dann*
	there	*dort*
	thin	*dünn*
	thing	*Ding, Sache*
to	**think**	*denken*
	third	*dritte / r / s*
	thirsty	*durstig*
	thirteen	*dreizehn*
	this time	*dieses Mal*
	those	*jene*
	thousand	*Tausend*
	three	*drei*
	through	*durch (hindurch)*
to	**throw**	*werfen*
to	**throw away sth.**	*etwas wegwerfen*
	thunder	*Donner*
	thunderstorm	*Gewitter*
	ticket	*Fahrkarte*
	time	*Zeit*
	tinny	*blechern*
	tiny	*winzig*
	title	*Titel*
	today	*heute*
	toddler	*Kleinkind (1 – 3 Jahre)*
	together	*zusammen*
	toilet	*Toilette*
	tomato (pl. tomatoes)	*Tomate*
	tonight	*heute Abend*
	too	*zu (+ Adjektiv)*
	tool	*Werkzeug*
	top	*Spitze*
	torch	*Fackel*

to	**touch**	*anfassen, berühren*
	touched	*bewegt*
	touristy	*touristenmäßig*
	towards	*in Richtung von*
	town	*Stadt*
	traditional	*traditionell*
	trail	*Pfad*
	train	*Zug*
to	**travel**	*reisen*
	tree	*Bäume*
to	**tremble**	*zittern*
	true	*wahr*
to	**try**	*versuchen*
to	**turn (around)**	*sich umdrehen*
to	**turn off**	*abschalten*
to	**turn on sth**	*etwas einschalten*
to	**turn out**	*sich herausstellen*
	turret	*Turm*
	twelve	*zwölf*
	twenty-ninth	*neunundzwanzigste/r/s*
	twice	*zweimal*
	two	*zwei*
	typical	*typisch*

U

	ugly	*hässlich*
	under	*unter*
	underneath	*unter*
to	**understand**	*verstehen*
	unfortunately	*unglücklicherweise, leider*
	unhappy	*traurig, unglücklich*
	unless	*wenn nicht*
to	**untie**	*lösen, losmachen*
	until	*bis*
	up	*auf, hinauf*
to	**use**	*benutzen*
	usually	*gewöhnlich*

V

	valley	*Tal*
	verdict	*Urteilsspruch*
	very	*sehr*
	victorious	*siegreich*
	view	*Sicht*
	village	*Dorf*
	violence	*Gewalt*
	visible	*sichtbar*
	voice	*Stimme*
	vomit	*Erbrochenes*

W

to	**wait**	*warten*
to	**wake sb.**	*jdn. wecken*
to	**walk**	*gehen*
to	**walk across sth.**	*über etw. gehen*
to	**walk away with**	*weglaufen mit*
	walking aid	*Gehhilfe*
	walks	*Spaziergänge*
	wall	*Mauer*
	wallet	*(AE) Geldbeutel*
to	**wander**	*ziellos umherstreifen*
to	**want**	*wollen*
	warm	*warm*
to	**warn**	*warnen*
	washing line	*Wäscheleine*
	watch	*Armbanduhr*
to	**watch**	*beobachten*
	water	*Wasser*
	waterfall	*Wasserfall*
	waters	*hier: Fruchtblase*
	way	*Weg; Art, Weise*
to	**wear**	*tragen (Kleidung)*
	weather	*Wetter*
	wedding anniversary	*Hochzeitstag*
	week	*Woche*
	weekend	*Wochenende*
to	**welcome sb.**	*jdn. willkommen heißen*
	welcoming	*freundlich*
	well-groomed	*gepflegt*
	Well, ...	*Also, ...; Äh, ...*
	wet	*nass*
	what	*was*
	whatever	*was auch immer*
	wheelchair	*Rollstuhl*

	when	*wenn, sobald*
	where	*wo*
	wherever	*wo auch immer*
	whether	*ob*
	which	*der / die / das, welche / r / s*
	while	*während*
to	**whisper**	*flüstern*
	white	*weiß*
	who	*wer, wen, wem*
	whom	*wen, wem*
	why	*warum*
	wife	*Ehefrau*
	wig	*Perücke*
	wind	*Wind*
	window	*Fenster*
	windscreen	*Windschutzscheibe*
	wine	*Wein*
to	**wipe**	*wischen*
	wire	*Draht*
	with	*mit*
	within	*innerhalb*
	without	*ohne*
	witness	*Zeuge, Zeugin*
to	**wobble**	*wackeln, schwanken*
	woman (pl. women)	*Frau*
	wonderful	*wunderbar*
to	**work**	*arbeiten*
	world	*Welt*
	worried	*besorgt*
to	**worry**	*sich sorgen*
	worse	*schlimmer / e / r / s*
to	**write**	*schreiben*
	writer	*Autor / in*
	wrong	*falsch*

Y

yard	*Yard (Längenmaß ca. 1 m)*
year	*Jahr*
yellow	*gelb*
yellowed	*vergilbt*
yesterday	*gestern*
young	*jung*

(Thomas Hartmann (Illustrathomas)): **5.6, 14, 77;** Fotolia, New York: **26.1** (wittayayut); **26.3** (rh2010); **55.2** (Rido); **92**, **99** (antiqueimages); **94.1** (asiastock); **94.2** (FotoKachna); **97.5** (Andrii IURLOV); **106.2** (rilueda); **113.1** (swisshippo); **113.2** (Janni); **113.4** (Leonid Ikan); **113.5** (Aikon); **126.1** (Andrey Kiselev); **170.1** (K. Thalhofer); **170.6** (marog-pixcells); iStockphoto, Calgary, Alberta: **10.1** (Lenorlux); **10.5** (donlucius); **11.2** (AVTG); **11.3** (tupungato); **11.4** (Jim_Pintar); **11.5** (LUHUANFENG); **61.5** (mikedabell); **74.1** (alvarez); **74.3** (pablohart); **74.4** (horstgerlach); **80.2** (borchee); **88** (christymon); **94.3** (lolostock); **94.4** (daverhead); **94.5** (VladCa); **95.1** (ProjectB); **95.2** (GuruJosh); **95.4** (Daniel_Kay); **97.3** (Image Source); **113.3** (TothGaborGyula); **119.2** (lostinbids); **119.5** (si_arts); **126.2** (Handemandaci); **126.5** (SolStock); **126.6** (NADOFOTOS); **132.3** (malerapaso); **132.4** (Floortje); **132.5** (scanrail); **132.6** (ahmetemre); **133.4** (YakobchukOlena); **133.5** (sqback); **139.1** (Andrew F Kazmierski); **139.3** (Geber86); **170.2** (wepix); **170.4** (Creativemarc); **170.5** (akurtz); **177.2** (GalDanieli); **177.3** (zhudifeng); **177.4** (NelleG); **177.5** (vicnt); **177.6** (KatarzynaBialasiewicz); **179.1** (McIninch); **179.2** (Neustockimages); **179.4** (Nerthuz); **179.5** (stockyimages); **179.6** (EdnaM); Shutterstock, New York: **5**, S.63 (Katja Gerasimova); **5**, S. 7 Dampflock, **82**, **87** (Aleks Melnik); **5** S.50 Dorf;, **6**, S.129 (Canicula); **5**,S. 36 Vollmond (Dimonika); **5**, S.22 (tony mills); **6**, S.91 (impress); **6**, S.109 (tapilipa); **6**, S.149 Justizia; S.151 Waage; S.154 Handschellen; S.156 Gestzesbuch; S.161 Hammer; (alex74); **6**, S.167 Haus; (alicedaniel); **8** (Enzo Molinari); **10.2** (Joseph Sohm); **10.4** (Northern Imaging); **10.6** (Aleksandr Pasechnik); **11.1** (photo.ua); **12**, S.15 Spinnennetz; S. 16, S. 19 Totenkopf; S. 17 Vampir; S. 18 Spinne mit Kreuz; S.20 Spinne mit Netz; (nubenamo); **21** (Brian Maudsley); **23** (Olga Tropinina); **25** gewellte Karte; S.27 Rucksack; S.28 Wegweiser; S.28 Fernglas; S. 29 Kompass; S.34 Karte gefaltet; (balabolka); **26.2** (oley); **26.4** (Anton Papulov); **26.5** (NadyaEugene); **26.6** (Voyagerix); **31** be prepared; (Ivan Baranov); **33** (reiza); **35** (Murray Golder); **39.1** (Andrey Arkusha); **39.3** (ERainbow); **39.4** (Roman Samborskyi); **39.5** (Nina Buday); **40.1** (andreiuc88); **40.2** (Byron Aguilar); **40.3** (Zacarias Pereira da Mata); **40.4** (Milosz_G); **40.5** (Sergei Kardashev); **43** stehender Geist; (olimpvector); **45** (Slava Gerj); **46** (Billy Stock); **51** (Olga Tropinina); **54** (Undrey); **58** Steinbrücke; S.60 einzelner Baum; S.53 Mauer mit Tor; (Rumdecor); **61.1** (Brent Hofacker); **61.2** (Africa Studio); **61.3** (Glynnis Jones); **61.4**, **61.6**, **80.1** (Bikeworldtravel); **64** (mtmmarek); **65**, S.67, S.73, S.75 Ornament (Vector Tradition SM); **66.1** (Lukasz Pajor); **66.2** (Nella); **66.3** (Mr. Sergey Olegovich); **66.4** (Deatonphotos); **66.5** (Michail Patakos); **66.6** (Simon Annable); **68.1**, **68.2**, **68.3**, **68.4**, **70.1**, **70.2**, **70.3** (kenkuza); **71** Pos.1 kurzes Masßband; S.71, Pos. 2, Zolstöcke; (pikepicture); **73.1** (basel101658); **74.2** (Willem Dijkstra); **74.5** (Stefano_Valeri); **74.6** (nadiya_sergey); **79** (Jim Francis); **80.3** (Sergio Stakhnyk); **80.4** (SJ Travel Photo and Video); **80.5** (Dusan Milenkovic); **80.6** (Carmina McConnell); **81.1** (MarkLG); **81.2** (Iain Frazer); **81.3** (Ruslan Ivantsov); **81.4** (Duncan Payne); **81.5** (Mmartin); **86** (Vector Draco); **90** (Rido); **93**, 100 Regenwolke (Multigon); **94.6** (Angela Schmidt); **95.3** (Anna Nikonorova); **95.5** (Sasa Prudkov); **97.1** (Soundsnaps); **97.2** (pixelheadphoto digitalskillet); **97.4** (Sawat Banyenngam); **106.1** (Palabra); **106.3** (Rido); **106.4** (Liderina); **110** (onot); **111**, S.112, S.113, S.114, S115 Schneeflocken; S.114 Geschenke; S.114 Tannenbaum; S.114, S.115, S. 117 Mistelzweig; (Elena Kazanskaya); **112.1** (Dmitry Kalinovsky); **112.2**, **133.3** (Andrey_Popov); **112.3** (Micha Rosenwirth); **112.4** (SKphotographer); **112.6** (Thiranun Kunatum); **117** Schnuller; S.118 Trinkflasche; S.118 Kinderwagen; S119 Schnabelflasche; S120 Mobile; S122 Schaukelpferd; S.122 Schaf; S.123 Dreirad; S.125 Storch; S.127 Schleife; (AuraLux); **119.1** (Tatiana Makotra); **119.3** (Oksana Kuzmina); **119.4** (Iulian Valentin); **119.6** (Bosko); **126.3** (pkproject); **126.4** (FamVeld); **130** (RomanYa); **131** Polizeiauto; S.140 Polizeimarke; S.145 Polizeimütze; S.147 Handschellen; (Macrovector); **132.1** (StudioSmart); **132.2** (MishAl); **133.1** (Morrowind); **133.2** (jannoon028); **135** (Bukhavets Mikhail); **139.2** (lazyllama); **139.4** (William Perugini); **139.5** (Monkey Business Images); **139.6** (a katz); **142** (Igor Sorokin); **150** (tokuze); **152**, S163, S.164, S.166 Blutflecken; (NIKHOM KEDBAN); **153** (yurchello108); **159** (P.S.Art-Design-Studio); **168.1** Spachtel; S.169 Hammer; S.169 Schrauben; S.169 Rolle; S.169 Pinsel; S.170 Wasserwaage; S.172 Schraubenzieher; S.171 Säge; S.171 Zange; (ArtAllAnd); **168.2** (Panda Vector); **175** (Elzbieta Sekowska); **177.1** (hkeita); **179.3** (StockLite); Thinkstock, München: **10.3** (cybrain); **11.6** (andylid); **39.2** (NinaMalyna); **55.1** (MilaSemenova); **81.6** (KOICHI SAITO/amanaimagesRF); **112.5** (andy0man); **170.3** (hikesterson); **171.1** (mbongorus); **171.2** (Zoonar/P. Malyshev); **171.3** (koya79); **171.4** (cherezoff); **171.5** (hehezhizhi); **171.6** (WoodyAlec)